HAM

HAMSTERS

The Complete Guide to Keeping, Breeding and Showing

JIMMY McKAY

BLANDFORD

To Jane, my wife, for all her support, encouragement and efforts, without which this book would never have appeared.

First published in the UK 1991 by Blandford, an imprint of Cassell plc, Wellington House, 125 Strand, London WC2R 0BB

First paperback edition 1995

Distributed in the United States by
Sterling Publishing Co., Inc.,
387 Park Avenue South, New York, NY 10016-8810

Distributed in Australia by
Capricorn Link (Australia) Pty Ltd,
2/13 Carrington Road, Castle Hill, NSW 2154

British Library Cataloguing in Publication Data
McKay, Jimmy
The new hamster handbook.
1. Pets. Hamsters. Care
I. Title
636.93233

ISBN 0-7137-2590-7

Typeset by Litho Link Ltd, Welshpool, Powys, Wales
Printed and bound in Great Britain by Biddles Ltd., Guildford and King's Lynn

Contents

Acknowledgements

Line illustrations: Jane McKay   pp.14, 27, 38, 44, 68 (bottom), 81, 82, 117

Black and white photographs: Jimmy McKay, except the following which appear by kind permission:

Baron's, London   p.15 (left)

The Natural History Museum, London   pp.10, 13

President and Council of The Royal Society, London   p.18

Professor Heinrich Mendelssohn, Department of Zoology, Tel-Aviv University   p.15 (right)

Colour photographs: Jimmy McKay

Introduction

Hamsters are one of today's most popular pets. They are of a size – 170mm (6¾in) – which is easily managed by children and adults alike. They do not possess the long tail of mice and rats (which many people do not like) and neither do they smell. Add to that the fact that the hamster, because of its food-storing habits (its name derives from the old German verb *hamstern* – 'to hoard'), can safely be left on its own while its owner has a weekend break, and it is easy to see why this animal is so popular.

The most commonly encountered species, and the subject of this book, is the so-called 'golden hamster' (*Mesocricetus auratus*). Today, because this species is now bred in such a wide variety of colours, it is usually referred to as the 'Syrian hamster', because of its country of origin.

To the small livestock fancier, the hamster offers all the challenges of the larger forms of exhibition animal, but at a greatly reduced cost. Due to its extremely short gestation period – a mere 16 days – it is also an ideal animal for the geneticist. For these (and other) reasons, the Syrian hamster has firmly established itself alongside the rabbit and the cavy as one of the most popular of the small exhibition animals.

When, shortly after World War 2, the hamster became both a popular pet and a favourite with small animal fanciers, the governing body of the Fancy in the U.K., the National Hamster Council (now known as the National Syrian Hamster Council – N.S.H.C.) encouraged two fanciers – Deaton and Pond – to produce a handbook that would benefit both beginner and experienced breeder alike, and help them to breed better hamsters and generally get more from their hobby. In 1956, *The Hamster Handbook* was published. The book attempted to supply the reader with the answers to almost every conceivable question on the subject. As such, the *Handbook* soon became the 'bible' of the Fancy, and was responsible for the introduction of many people (including myself) to the hobby of hamster breeding and exhibiting.

Today, over 30 years later, *The Hamster Handbook* is long out of print and has become something of a collector's item. The book still holds a special place in the hearts of all of those who used it all those years ago, perhaps because there has never been another book to take its place. This, *The New Hamster Handbook*, has been written with this in mind.

I have attempted to give all the information that a newcomer to the Fancy could wish to have but, until now, has been unable to find in a single volume. It is also hoped that the contents will be of interest to the established fancier/breeder, as all the latest thinking has been incorporated into the text. This includes the use of new technology and a chapter on judging since, although not everyone will aspire to being a show judge, a knowledge of the principles involved will be extremely beneficial to all intending to bench their stock.

I was very lucky to have had the guidance of an extremely experienced and highly respected hamster breeder/exhibitor during my early, formative years in the Fancy, in the person of Don Baxby. I hope that some of the sage advice that he gave to me will, through the pages of this book, be passed on to yet another generation of hamster fanciers.

This book also contains the full and accurate story of the discovery of the Syrian hamster and its subsequent introduction to the pet and Fancy market. This is the culmination of many months of research and it is – as far as I can tell – the first time ever that this story has been told in a single volume. I have also managed to track down photographs of some of the individuals involved in this story. My research has proved that many 'facts' previously published by some authorities were not true: many were exaggerated, some were clearly false.

Throughout the book, I refer to all fanciers and breeders in the male form. I am well aware that there are many females (both young and not so young) who are active hamster breeders and exhibitors, but use this approach because it is necessary to have some consistency in my writings.

My research on this subject has been helped immensely by the staff of the libraries of the Natural History Museum and the Zoological Society of London. In particular, I must thank Sue Bevis for all her efforts and encouragement.

The production of this book would not have been possible without the encouragement and support that I have received from my wife, Jane, who allowed me to escape my decorating duties to prepare the manuscript and carry out my research. Thank you.

Sincere thanks to Noel Walker, M.R.C.V.S., who very kindly checked, added to and commented on the chapter covering disease and injuries in hamsters; and to Anne Dray, who checked and commented on the chapter on hamster genetics.

I must also thank all of my friends in the Hamster Fancy, some of whom are to be seen in the photographs in this volume. They have had to contend with my near-impossible demands to ensure that I obtained the photographs and information which I required.

I have also received much encouragement and assistance from my fellow fanciers, and I hope this book is not a disappointment to them.

Jimmy McKay

George Robert Waterhouse, Curator of the Zoological Society of London, who first presented an elderly female specimen of the golden hamster to a meeting of the Society on 9 April 1839.

CHAPTER 1

Origins

Almost every book written on the subject of the Syrian hamster has a section on the history of the animal's origins, discovery and subsequent introduction to the pet and Fancy arena. I make no apologies for including such a section in this book. Having read almost every book on the subject, I came to the conclusion that none had got all of the story correct, as many contradicted other accounts, while some were obviously verbatim copies of previously published histories. I therefore decided to go back to basics and research the *original* documents. I also communicated with many of the people involved in the story or, where this was impossible for various reasons, with their close relatives and colleagues, in order to ensure that I had the true facts and figures. I am confident, therefore, that what follows is the *real* story of the origins and discovery of the Syrian hamster told in full for the first time.

HISTORY

The first recorded human encounter with the golden hamster was in 1797, in the second edition of a book entitled *The Natural History of Aleppo*, by a physician called Alexander Russell (with additional notes by Patrick, Alexander's younger brother). As this second edition was published after Alexander's death, it is possible that the golden hamster was not discovered by Alexander, but by Patrick, although I can find no other evidence to support this theory. The following is an extract from the book:

> The hamster is less common than the field mouse. I once found, upon dissecting one of them [a hamster], the pouch on each side [of the head] stuffed with young French beans, arranged lengthwise so exactly, and so close to each other, that it appeared strange by what mechanism it had been effected; for the membrane which forms the pouch, through muscular, is thin, and the most expert fingers could not have packed the beans in more regular order. When they were laid loosely on the table, they formed a heap three times the bulk of the animal's body.

The book does not claim that this was a newly discovered species; the author seems to have assumed that the hamster in question was a member of the species then known as *Mus cricetus*, and now known as *Cricetus cricetus* (the common, or European hamster). It was not until 1839 that the species was recognized as being separate from the European hamster.

George Robert Waterhouse, while curator of the Zoological Society of London, presented a rather elderly female specimen (received from Aleppo, Syria, from an unacknowledged source) to a meeting of the Society on 9 April 1839. In 1840, Waterhouse's description of the specimen was published in the *Proceedings of the Zoological Society*:

> This species is less [smaller] than the common hamster (*Cricetus vulgaris*) [this is no longer the scientific name], and is remarkable for its deep golden colouring. The fur is moderately long, and very soft, and has a silk-like gloss; the deep golden yellow colouring extends over the upper parts and sides of the head and body, and also over the outer sides of the limbs. On the back, the hairs are brownish at the tips, hence in this part, the fur assumes a deeper hue than on the sides of the body. The sides of the muzzle, throat and under parts of the body are white, but faintly tinted with yellow. On the back and sides of the body, all the hairs are of a deep grey or lead colour at the base, and on the under parts of the body, the hairs are indistinctly tinted with grey at the base. The feet and tail are white. The ears are of moderate size, furnished externally with deep golden-coloured hairs, and internally with whitish hairs. Moustaches are of black and white hairs mixed.

This 'new' species was named *Cricetus auratus* Waterhouse, and the actual specimen is still kept at the Natural History Museum, as Item BM(NH) 1855. 12. 24. 120. This specimen lacks the markings and ticking that most people expect to see in a modern hamster.

The specimen is also somewhat smaller than today's hamster. The skull (also preserved in the Natural History Museum as Item BM(NH) 1119a) measures 40mm (1%16in) long and 17mm (1^{1}/16in) wide, with the cheek bones measuring 23mm (⅞in) between the outer edges.

In 1880, a former Consul-General at Aleppo, James Henry Skene, brought a colony of golden hamsters back to his home in Edinburgh, Scotland. He had caught and bred these animals while serving in Aleppo. This colony survived for over 30 years, and was probably the first instance of live golden hamsters being kept in the U.K.

In the late 1920s, Saul Adler, the Professor of Parasitology at the Hebrew University of Jerusalem, was looking for an endemic hamster species for his research on the disease leishmaniasis (oriental sore), as the Chinese hamsters (*Cricetulus griseus*) that he was using were proving difficult to breed, and he was not prepared to rely solely on imports of the animal from its native area. So interested and

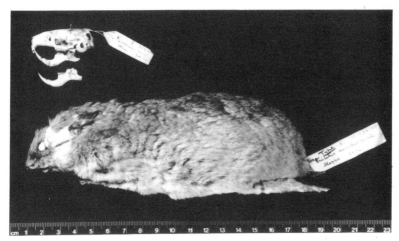

The remains of the specimen that Waterhouse presented to the Zoological Society of London in 1839. This became the 'type specimen', and can still be viewed in the Natural History Museum, Cromwell Road, London, England.

eminent in this field of studies was Adler, that he was appointed to take charge of the Kala-azar Commission of the Royal Society between 1931 and 1934.

Born in Karelitz, U.S.S.R., in 1895, Adler's family emigrated to the U.K. in 1900. Saul was educated in Leeds, first at the Gower Street Board School, from where, in 1906, he won a scholarship to Leeds Central High School. In 1912, Adler gained a medical scholarship to Leeds University and qualified in 1917, at which time he took a commission in the Royal Army Medical Corps, and was posted to Mesopotamia, where he served until 1920. When he left the army, he joined the Liverpool School of Tropical Medicine. Between 1921 and 1924, Adler worked in the Sir Alfred Lewis Jones laboratory, in Sierra Leone, as a research assistant.

In 1923, Saul Adler married a girl of Russian–Jewish extraction, Sophie Husden, who later bore him three children – two sons and a daughter. Adler was appointed as the assistant in the microbiological department of the Hebrew University of Jerusalem, in 1924, and became the associate Professor of Parasitology in 1928, and Professor of Parasitology in 1934. He held this latter post until his death in 1966.

While at the Hebrew University, Adler was always looking for 'new' species of animals to use in his research, and is said to have known of the existence of the golden hamster, through Waterhouse's paper, and so it may be that he deliberately wished to capture this particular species. Consequently, Adler asked a member of the university's zoology department, Israel Aharoni, to help him obtain some of these indigenous hamsters.

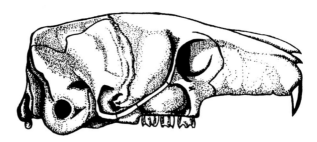

Fig. 1 Skull of hamster. Notice the perpetually growing and self-sharpening teeth.

Born in the Russian/Polish border town of Widzi, Aharoni was orphaned at an early age and raised by his grandparents. Up to the age of 14 years, he studied in a *yeshiva*, and his tutors there thought of him as a child prodigy. He then decided that he should move on and ran away to Prague, equipped with six books – a Bible, three zoology books by Mendele Mokher, a German–Russian dictionary, and a Hebrew–German dictionary.

He enrolled at the University of Prague, where he studied zoology and Semitic philology, expressing a special interest in the animal life of the Middle East. He was also extremely interested in the names of animals as they appeared in the Bible, the Talmud, and other ancient literature. While at this univesity, Aharoni also mastered several languages.

It was not too long before Israel Aharoni decided that it was time to move on again, expressing his belief that the animal life of the Holy Land must be studied *in situ*, and consequently he left the University of Prague (before he had completed his studies) and went to Palestine, arriving in April 1902 and settling in the town of Rehovot, where he founded its first elementary school.

He later married Judith Goldin, the daughter of the Mayor of Rehovot, and then moved to Jerusalem, where he spent hour after hour researching and studying in the libraries of the Dominican and Franciscan institutions in the Old City. He founded a zoological museum at the Bezalel Art School, and was appointed its curator.

Aharoni soon became renowned as an eminent zoologist, and he accompanied many research expeditions sponsored (and protected) by Abdul-Hamid, the Turkish Sultan, spending many months studying the desert areas of Iraq, southern Transjordan and Syria. During this time in the desert, he made friends with the Bedouin tribesmen, and was regularly accompanied by Yehezkel, who was searching for the ten lost tribes of Israel.

Left Saul Adler, Professor of Parasitology at the Hebrew University of Jerusalem, who commissioned Israel Aharoni to capture specimens of the golden hamster in 1930. Adler needed these animals, which he had become aware of through Waterhouse's paper, to use in his research on the disease leishmaniasis.

Right Israel Aharoni, the leader of the expedition which captured wild golden hamsters *(Mesocricetus auratus)* in a field near Aleppo, Syria. He and his wife had to raise the litter after the mother hamster began killing her offspring.

During World War 1, Aharoni served in the Turkish army as its official zoologist, and, in 1915, he was sent by the army to establish a zoological museum in Damascus, being transferred later to Qasra, near Zahleh, in Lebanon. After the war, he returned to Palestine, then under British rule, where the British Mandate government employed him as a zoologist. When the Hebrew University was founded, he was appointed as the head of its Department of Zoology and its zoological museum. He continued working there, assisted by his daughter Bat-Sheva, until his death in 1946. Bat-Sheva wrote a biography of her father, but this has never been published.

During his life, Aharoni published many articles (in many different languages) and a whole series of zoologicial textbooks, covering mammals, birds and reptiles. His most famous book was entitled *Memoirs of a Hebrew Zoologist*, and contains detailed and fascinating accounts (in Hebrew) of his expeditions and work in Palestine, including reports on many of the rare animals that he collected. These included the Syrian bear, the Syrian ostrich and the oryx. He also allotted Hebrew names to the wildlife of Palestine, based on his studies and research of Hebrew and Arabic sources, and being guided by many locals. Indeed, he often described his greatest wish – that the fauna of the Holy Land be studied by Jewish scholars, living in that country, who would also conduct in-depth studies of various species, including their ecology. It is befitting that he became known as 'the first Hebrew Zoologist'.

In 1930, accompanied by a local guide (Georgius Khalil Tah'an), Aharoni set out to search for hamsters in the Aleppo region of Syria, and he included an account of this expedition in his memoirs, published in 1942 (*Memoirs of a Hebrew Zoologist*). Both Aharoni and his guide knew of the existence of the golden hamster and they entreated Sheik El-Beled, the local sheik, to help them find some.

On the Sheik's instructions, local villagers set about the task of digging for hamsters in the surrounding wheatfields on 12 April 1930. In one hole, 2.5m (8ft) deep, they found a complete nest containing a female and 11 pups (babies) still with their eyes closed. The entire nest – pups, mother and all – was placed in a wooden box when disaster struck. Aharoni graphically describes in his memoirs the way in which the mother destroyed one of her pups by biting off its head. When Georgius saw this, he quickly removed the mother in order to save the rest of the litter. He then disposed of the mother by placing her in a killing-jar containing cyanide. (Aharoni later captured more golden hamsters, on 27 and 29 April 1930, and the remains of the three adult female specimens owned by, and exhibited in, the Berlin Zoological Museum, are credited to him.)

One of the pups escaped but the other nine were successfully hand-reared by Aharoni and his wife, and the litter was given to Dr Hein Ben-Menachen, back at the Hebrew University, who placed them in a wooden-floored cage at the University's animal breeding centre, on Mount Scopus. Next day, he discovered that the hamsters had gnawed a hole in the cage, and five had escaped. None of these escapees was recovered alive. According to Professor Aharoni, this left three males and a single female, but other reports conflict with this. However, within a year of being bred in captivity, the hamsters (now secured in a large wire-mesh cage packed tightly with hay) produced 150 young! Some of the first progeny were given to Saul Adler, who later published the first report on their use in research.

Realizing that having only a single colony of this 'new' animal was very dangerous, Adler decided to distribute some stock to scientists in other areas. In 1931, Adler brought two pairs of hamsters to the U.K. (he smuggled them in tucked in the pockets of his coat!), and these were presented to Professor Edward Hindle, at the Wellcome Bureau of Scientific Research, in London.

Edward Hindle was born in Sheffield on 21 March 1886; his family originated in Lancashire, but his grandfather, James, took the family to Wirksworth, Derbyshire, and his own father then moved to Sheffield.

Edward's mother, Sarah, was a qualified teacher and Edward, his brother and four sisters were all educated at home. Edward's interest in nature soon showed and his mother encouraged him in this. He later attended classes at the Bradford Technical College and, in 1903, he was awarded a scholarship at the Royal College of Science, in South Kensington, London.

Hindle successfully sat his Associateship in Zoology in 1906, at which time his family emigrated to California. After a year as a research assistant at the Liverpool School of Tropical Medicine, Hindle joined his family in California, and spent six months at the Marine Biological Station at La Jolla, before enrolling at the University of Berkeley. He obtained his Ph.D. from that university in 1910, returning to the U.K. in the same year.

Back in England, he went to the Magdalene College of the University of Cambridge, and took a degree in the Natural Science Tripos (B.A. 1912; M.A. 1917), and became Sc.D. in 1926. In later life, he became intimately associated with both the Glasgow and London Zoological Gardens.

A territorial soldier, Hindle volunteered for regular army service at the outbreak of World War 1, being gazetted, on 1 October 1914, to the Royal Engineers as a Second Lieutenant. He served in France and Palestine, returning to the U.K. in late 1917, where he took command of the newly formed Signal Service Training Unit for Officers. He went back to Palestine in 1918, later moving to Egypt, from where he was demobilized in 1919.

As the threat of war loomed again in 1938, Hindle, now Regius Professor of Zoology at Glasgow University, played an active part in the Officers' Training Corps at that university. He became a Lieutenant Colonel (General List) and commanding officer of the whole Corps, being appointed as Secretary of the Reception Unit for recruitment of officers in the west of Scotland. He also commanded the 14th Battalion, City of Glasgow, Home Guard.

He founded the Zoological Society of Glasgow in 1939, acquiring Calder Park for the site of the zoological gardens. He left the area in 1944 to join the Zoological Society of London.

In 1928, Hindle was appointed as the Beit Research Fellow in Tropical Medicine at the Wellcome Bureau of Scientific Research, where he carried out research on leishmaniasis.

When able to do so, Hindle successfully bred the hamsters both in London and at the University of Glasgow. He published a paper in 1934, in conjunction with Miss H.M. Bruce, describing them in detail, as follows:

The Golden Hamster is smaller than the common European Hamster, a full grown female rarely exceeding a length of seven inches (180mm), and has a deep golden brown colour, but towards the roots the hairs are dark grey. The fur is short, soft, and smooth. The ventral surface is very light grey, with white patches. The ears are large, grey and almost naked, with a few golden brown hairs on the surface. The eyes are large and black. The skin is extremely loose, to such an extent that folds at least two inches (50mm) can be pulled out from any part of the trunk. The short stumpy tail, and especially the feet, are lighter in colour than the rest of the body. The cheek pouches are well developed, and can hold a surprisingly large amount of food. According to B. Aharoni (1932), these hamsters live in deep burrows which they make in grain fields. Although in nature they are presumably herbivorous, in captivity they are omnivorous, and, in addition to grain, will feed on roots, nuts, bread, meat, etc, and will carry off and store almost any portable object.

The tendency to store food is more strongly developed in the female than the male, and this instinct is present at a very early age, since young only two or three weeks old may be observed filling their pouches.

On 8 April 1932, Professor Hindle sent a few pairs of hamsters to London Zoo, where staff bred them so successfully that some surplus stock was sold to the general public (in 1937). In 1938, a small colony was exported from the U.K. to the U.S.A., where they were initially bred for laboratory use, but later surplus stock found its way to the

Professor Edward Hindle who, while working at the Wellcome Bureau of Scientific Research in London, England, in 1931, was given two pairs of hamsters by Saul Adler. Adler is reputed to have smuggled the animals into the U.K. in the pocket of his coat! Hindle successfully bred these hamsters and, almost exactly 93 years after Waterhouse had described the hamster to the Zoological Society of London, he presented live specimens to the Society at London Zoo. The progeny of these were eventually sold to the general public for the first time in 1937.

public in that country. Earlier that same year, however, Dr Adler had already sent a small colony of 13 hamsters to the Department of Hygiene and Bacteriology of the Western Reserve School of Medicine, Cleveland, U.S.A. This colony may well have arrived in the States via Professor I.J. Kliger, who had received his stock (in India) directly from Dr Adler.

In May/June 1971, an American, Michael Murphy, captured 13 golden hamsters in the Aleppo area and transported 12 of them (four males and eight females) back to the U.S.A. He states that, within three days of careful and gentle handling, all the hamsters were quite tame. All of the animals were mated within four weeks of capture, and all of the females produced and weaned litters, the average litter size being 11. The descendants of these animals are now being bred at the National Institute of Health in Bethesda, Maryland, U.S.A.

In 1978, another American, Bill Duncan, captured five golden hamsters in the Aleppo area, and returned to the South Western Medical School, Dallas, Texas, with two females.

In 1980, two golden hamsters were found by a rodent control officer working in Syria at the International Centre for Agricultural Research in the Dry Areas. Unfortunately, they both died shortly after capture, apparently because they ingested rat poison prior to their capture. The same man captured another pair at the same site in 1982, but the male died shortly afterwards. The female was imported into the U.K., but never bred (possibly because she was too old).

Although most hamster books state categorically that all of the Syrian hamsters in captivity are direct descendants of those found in 1930, those found in the 1970s and later have also contributed to the captive stock. Certainly, though, it is true that all captive hamsters *prior* to 1971 *did* originate from the litter found by Aharoni.

THE U.K. HAMSTER FANCY

By 1945, at the end of World War 2, the golden hamster had become a favourite pet in Britain. That same year saw two very important milestones for the Hamster Fancy in the U.K.: the British Hamster Club was formed and, in December, hamsters were exhibited for the very first time, at the Bradford Championship Show.

In 1948, it was felt that it would be beneficial to the Fancy if there was more than the one club. Consequently, two more clubs – the Midland and Northern Hamster Club, and the Kent and Southern Hamster Club – were formed, both under the auspices of the National Hamster Council. In 1949, the Fancy saw a great surge in interest, with the number of members multiplying several times during that year.

In 1949, fanciers in Yorkshire decided that they wanted their own club and, at a meeting in Harrogate on 10 December 1949, 34 Yorkshire hamster fanciers formed the Yorkshire Hamster Club (Y.H.C.). It was originally proposed that membership of the Y.H.C. be restricted to those fanciers resident in that county. However, the meeting decided that they would admit to membership anyone with a geniune interest in the hamster. The Yorkshire Hamster Club existed until 1987, when members voted to change its name to 'The Northern Hamster Club', to better reflect the area over which the Club had jurisdiction at that time (the whole of northern England, the whole of Scotland and Northern Ireland).

The British Hamster Fancy has continued to prosper, and today there are three main hamster clubs in the U.K. – Midland, Northern and Southern – and many more smaller groups, known as hamster circles. All of these operate under the auspices of the National Syrian Hamster Council (N.S.H.C.), a body consisting of elected officials plus representatives from all three clubs. It is the role of the Council to agree standards for each variety of hamster, to appoint N.S.H.C. Recognized Judges, and to generally guide the clubs.

Although local clubs stage hamster shows in many parts of the world, very few of these clubs have become as organized as those in the U.K., where the Hamster Fancy has a history almost as long as that of the hamster in captivity. Consequently, most clubs outside the U.K. adopt and/or adapt the standards, rules and regulations of the U.K.'s National Syrian Hamster Council and its affiliated clubs. Many of the standards are somewhat vague, and are therefore open to many interpretations. Readers who wish further clarification on any of these points should contact their own local club. Some of the varieties are also known by different names in some countries, although it is hoped that those given here, and used for many years in the U.K. Hamster Fancy, will be easily recognizable to the reader in other countries.

There are several names that are inextricably linked with the Hamster Fancy in the U.K. H.W. Reynolds is credited with writing the first booklet on the golden hamster (*Golden Hamsters*) in 1947. This small booklet consisted of 32 pages of basic facts about the keeping, breeding and exhibiting of the hamster, along with a very brief story of its discovery. The booklet had a foreword by Edward Hindle, and was sold mainly through zoos. In 1954, the Zoological Society of London acquired the copyright to the booklet and, in March of that year, issued the revised fourth edition of the book.

In 1956, two experienced and enthusiastic fanciers – Harry Deaton and T.W. ('Bob') Pond – wrote *The Hamster Handbook*. Pond published a paperback version of this book in 1962 through his own 'Pond Press', on behalf of the National Hamster Council.

Former N.H.C. President Percy 'Mr Hamster' Parslow is a name

The cover of the first published booklet on *Golden Hamsters*.

that, even many years after his death in the early 1980s, is still widely known and frequently mentioned in the Hamster Fancy. He began with hamsters in 1943, in Kingston, Surrey, eventually setting up the first 'Hamster Farm' in Great Bookham, Leatherhead, Surrey, on 23 October 1961. At this 3-acre farm, he bred countless thousands of hamsters, including the first tortoiseshell-and-white (1962). He wrote a book, *Percy Parslow's Hamsters in Colour*, in April 1967, following it with *The Basic Facts of Practical Hamster Breeding*, in November 1967. In 1969, he wrote *Hamsters*, a book which rapidly established itself as one of the best books in the early 1970s. I bought my first exhibition standard stock from Percy (via British Rail) in 1970. Prior to that, I had been keeping and breeding pet-shop quality hamsters.

The cover of the original *The Hamster Handbook* (paperback edition), by Deaton and Pond, which was responsible for establishing the hamster as a Fancy (exhibition) animal in the U.K.

Bob and Jean Parlett, the two longest-serving members of the British Hamster Fancy.

Two fanciers who are still active today – both well-respected judges and exhibitors – and who started their hamstering careers in 1947, are Bob and Jean Parlett. Based in the Midlands area of the U.K., these two stalwarts have been – and continue to be – the backbone of the Fancy there. Bob has been both N.H.C. President and Vice President, and has held many offices in the Midland Hamster Club, while Jean has also held numerous offices both at national and regional levels. Their expertise and wisdom is still called on today to help keep the Fancy on an even keel.

One of the first people to take a serious interest in hamster genetics was Roy Robinson, and he has published many works on this subject, including a chapter in *The Golden Hamster: its Biology and Use in Medical Research*, and *Colour Inheritance in Small Livestock*. Roy continues to work on this subject and his articles appear regularly in the specialist press.

The cover of *The Hamster Manual*, by Albert Marsh. This book helped popularize the golden hamster in the U.S.A.

HAMSTERS IN THE U.S.A.

In the U.S.A., Albert Marsh was probably more responsible than any other person for the hamster's success as a pet. Prior to acquiring his first hamster stock, Marsh was an unemployed highway engineer. He won his first hamster as the result of a bet and became fascinated by the species. He then obtained breeding stock from the leprosy laboratories in Carville, Louisiana, at which time he began to breed them in earnest and actively to promote the animal as both the perfect pet and laboratory animal.

He founded the Gulf Hamstery at 1514 Basil Street, Mobile, Alabama, and in 1948 self-published *The Hamster Manual*. According to his own records, this book sold 10,000 copies in just 6 months, with 40,000 copies being sold by April 1949, and 80,000 by 1951! He advertised regularly in comic books, magazines and commercial animal-breeders' journals.

Unfortunately for Marsh, many other people also realized the commercial potential of these wonderful little animals, and dozens of other hamsteries were formed throughout the U.S.A., with smaller and more localized breeders supplying the vast bulk of hamsters required by the pet trade. Consequently, the Gulf Hamstery went out of business in the mid-1950s, leaving behind the hamster as one of the most popular small pets in the U.S.A.

THE SWEDISH HAMSTER FANCY

In the early 1980s, hamster fanciers in Sweden joined together to form the 'Svenska Hamster Foreningens' (S.H.F., the Swedish Hamster Society). Since then, they have organized themselves to a very high standard, in many ways better and more refined than that of the U.K.

Realizing that the breeding of consistently good animals depended on accurate record keeping by all concerned, they introduced mandatory registration of every hamster which was to be exhibited, in much the same way as the dog Fancy operates throughout the world. Consequently, the national organizer keeps a record of every hamster, its breeder, its owner, every pup that it either sires or gives birth to, and every result of every show that it enters. Every hamster sold must be accompanied by its pedigree, giving all the above details and listing all ancestors for the last three generations.

When a hamster is judged to be worthy, it is awarded a 'Certificate' by the judge at that show. When it has been awarded three of these certificates, it becomes a 'Champion'. Recognizing that hamsters develop with age, the society also holds specific classes for hamsters aged between two and five months.

The Swedish Society holds the U.K. Fancy in high regard, and regularly invites British judges to preside over their shows, an honour that has been bestowed upon the author. No one visiting a Swedish Hamster Society show can fail to be impressed by the sheer dedication and professionalism exhibited by all of those involved. Other countries should look to the S.H.F., and follow their lead if the Hamster Fancy is to be more widely accepted worldwide.

SCIENTIFIC CLASSIFICATION

The Syrian (golden) hamster is a rodent and is zoologically classified as follows:

Phylum   Chordata (possesses a spinal cord).

Class   Mammalia (has hair, gives birth to live young, nurses young, warm-blooded, etc.).

Order   Rodentia (possesses perpetually-growing and self-sharpening teeth).

Sub-order   Myomorpha (mouse-like rodents).

Family   Cricetidae (hamsters and voles).

Sub-family Cricetinae (hamsters).

Genus   *Mesocricetus* (middle-sized hamsters).

Species   *auratus* (golden-coloured).

Classification of rodents*

Order RODENTIA
Rodents: 3 sub-orders, 30 families, 389 genera, 1702 species.

Sub-order SCIUROMORPHA
Squirrel-like rodents: 7 families, 65 genera, 377 species.

Families:
Castoridae (beavers): 1 genus, 2 species.
Aplodontidae (mountain beaver): 1 genus, 1 species.
Anomaluridae (scaly-tailed squirrels): 3 genera, 7 species.
Sciuridae (squirrels): 49 genera, 267 species.
Geomyidae (pocket gophers): 5 genera, 34 species.
Heteromyidae (pocket mice): 5 genera, 65 species.
Pedetidae (springhares): 1 genus, 1 species.

Sub-order MYOMORPHA
Mouse-like rodents: 5 families, 264 genera, 1137 species.

Families:
Muridae (rats and mice): 15 sub-families, 241 genera, 1082 species.
Gliridae, Seleviniidae (dormice): 8 genera, 11 species.
Zapodidae (jumping mice and birch mice): 4 genera, 14 species.
Dipodidae (jerboas): 11 genera, 31 species.

Sub-order CAVIAMORPHA
Cavy-like Rodents: 18 families, 59 genera, 188 species.

Families:
Erethizontidae (New World porcupines): 4 genera, 10 species.
Caviidae (cavies): 5 genera, 14 species.
Hydrochoeridae (capybara): 1 genus, 1 species.
Myocastoridae (coypu): 1 genus, 1 species.
Capromyidae (hutias): 4 genera, 13 species.
Dinomyidae (pacarana): 1 genus, 1 species.
Agoutidae (pacas): 1 genus, 2 species.
Dasyproctidae (agoutis and acouchis): 2 genera, 13 species.
Abrocomidae (chinchilla rats): 1 genus, 2 species.
Echimyidae (spiny rats): 15 genera, 55 species.
Chinchillidae (chinchillas and viscachas): 3 genera, 6 species.
Octodontidae (degus): 5 genera, 8 species.
Ctenomyidae (tuco-tucos): 1 genus, 33 species.
Thryonomyidae (cane rats): 1 genus, 2 species.
Petromyidae (African rock rat): 1 genus, 1 species.
Hystricidae (Old World porcupines): 4 genera, 11 species.
Ctenodactylidae (gundis): 4 genera, 5 species.
Bathyergidae (African mole-rats): 5 genera, 9 species.

*Based on the classification used by Dr David MacDonald in the *Encyclopedia of Mammals*.

The sub-family Cricetinae (hamsters)

The Cricetinae, which consist of five genera and 24 species, are found in Europe, the Middle East, the U.S.S.R. and China, inhabiting arid and semi-arid areas, varying from cultivated fields to mountain slopes

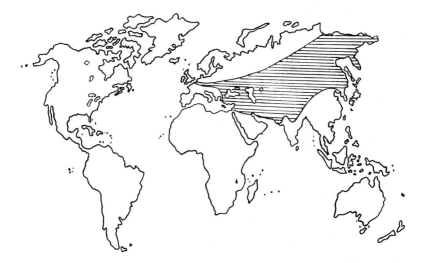

Fig. 2 World distribution of hamsters (shaded area).

and steppes. The smallest member of this sub-family is the Dzungarian dwarf hamster (*Phodopus sungorus*), which has a head-and-body length of 53–102mm (2¹⁄₁₆–4in), a tail length of 7–11mm (¼–⁷⁄₁₆in), and weighs about 50g (1¾oz). The largest member is the black-bellied (or common) hamster (*Cricetus cricetus*), which measures 200–280mm (7⅞–11¼in) along the head and body, has no tail to speak of, and weighs up to 920g (32½oz).

Members of this sub-family include the mouse-like hamster (*Cricetus bailwardi*), the Korean grey rat (*Cricetus triton*), the common or European hamster (*Cricetus cricetus*), the Dzungarian dwarf hamster (*Phodopus sungorus*) and, of course, the Syrian hamster (*Mesocricetus auratus*).

Characteristics

All hamsters possess a pair of cheek pouches that are quite capable of holding vast amounts of food. Indeed, the name hamster derives from an old German word meaning 'to hoard'. In Germany, hamsters (not the golden type that we shall be discussing in this volume, but the common or European hamster *Cricetus cricetus*) are regarded as pests, because they steal and hoard huge quantities of grain and other such foods; one recorded instance states that farmers discovered a hamster's food store weighing in at almost a quarter of a tonne! Not bad for a creature weighing less than one kilogram! This storing habit is very useful for the owner who has to go away for a weekend, as hamsters are quite capable of being left (provided that they are given sufficient food for their store), because they will feed themselves from this store.

A German hamster trap. In mainland Europe, where the common hamster is considered an agricultural pest, such traps are set in the tunnels of the hamster's home, and the animal sets them off when it pushes against the circular trip, which blocks its way.

Hamsters are naturally curious and make ideal pets.

Hamsters are often referred to as nocturnal, i.e. animals of the night. This is incorrect. They are actually crepuscular – creatures of dawn and dusk. As such, they make perfect pets, as they are active at the times that most people (both children and adults) are themselves active in the human home.

Being desert animals, hamsters do not drink much water (although in captivity they must be provided with a constant supply of fresh, clean water). This means that they do not urinate too often, nor in copious amounts – traits that give many advantages to the keeper of these animals, not least of which is the lack of the smell that always accompanies large amounts of urine. They also use the same spot for their 'toilet' – in captivity, this is almost always the furthest point from their nest area. Hamsters are almost totally without any smell of their own, which makes them ideal pets for those living in flats or other small abodes.

Much of the hamster's food requires opening, and so they have evolved dexterous paws with which to manipulate the seeds and nuts. This is just one of the many endearing characteristics of the animal. They also use these paws to perform their almost non-stop toilet – washing every bit of their bodies and grooming their fur to a silky sheen.

The word 'hamster' comes from the old German word *hamstern*, meaning 'to hoard'. Hamsters use their cheek pouches to transport food to their stores. This one is busy pouching acorns.

The Syrian hamster is extremely hardy, being able to withstand very low temperatures, provided that it is not subjected to damp and/ or draughts, and has sufficient bedding to build its nest. As the temperature drops, the hamster will increase the thickness of its nest and gradually make it into an almost solid sphere, with just enough room to enter and leave. As the temperature rises, the nest will then be opened up.

All hamsters are extremely shortsighted, and rely on their other senses to compensate for this. Their pinnae (ear flaps) are very large in comparison with the size of the head, and are held erect to funnel in sound, in much the same way as old-fashioned 'hearing trumpets' did.

While all of the foregoing characteristics are good reasons for keeping Syrian hamsters as pets, probably the most important characteristics for the keen fancier are the hamster's longevity and its gestation period.

With a gestation period (pregnancy) of between 15 and 17 days, the Syrian hamster has one of the shortest gestation periods known. While it is certainly not to be recommended, hamsters are physically capable of delivering their first litter at about 50 days old! This litter could be as small as a single pup (baby) or as large as over 20! One of my hamsters successfully reared 23 pups in 1987. The average litter is six pups.

Their fast breeding abilities plus their quite short life expectancy (2–3 years) mean that no hamster can reign supreme in the exhibition field for too long, while winning lines can be developed within a few months (see Chapter 5, Breeding), and new colour varieties can also be produced (see Chapter 6, Genetics).

Today, there are almost 30 recognized colour varieties, all of which can be bred with one (or more) of the four coat types (see Chapter 6, Genetics), giving fanciers and pet-keepers plenty of choice.

Breeding a winning hamster (or, even better, a winning line) is just as difficult, but as satisfying, as producing a winner at Crufts dog show or a horse to win the Grand National. Hamsters are, however, far cheaper to buy, house and feed!

Hamsters have so much to offer that there is little wonder that they are so popular as pets and exhibition animals and that, for some (myself included), they have become almost an obsession.

CHAPTER 2

Selection of Stock

The selection of one's initial stock is the most important decision that any hamster breeder will ever take. The quality of this stock will be reflected for the duration of the hamstery. The old adage 'act in haste, repent at leisure' is well worth remembering. The object of acquiring one's initial stock must be to obtain a nucleus around which a successful hamstery can be built. One does not want to have to keep buying fresh stock every year or so. Indeed, the hope is that the serious breeder can create a self-sustaining population of hamsters and only needs to acquire new stock when he desires to breed a different variety. A fancier will, nevertheless, still obtain the occasional outcross to inject hybrid vigour into his line.

The first decision that the potential hamster fancier must make is which variety to select. I say 'variety' rather than 'varieties' deliberately. Many tyros elect to breed several varieties from day one, and then discover that they do not possess the time, space or funds to keep the operation running at this level. For every variety chosen, a *minimum* of ten individuals must be kept at any one time in order to ensure that there will always be suitable stock to show and breed *and* be successful. In reality, this means that breeders will have up to 30 or 40 hamsters at one time (this figure includes pups and young hamsters). When selecting which pups to keep from any litter, many breeders keep two or three and 'run them on', which basically means that they keep them until the hamsters are about 12-15 weeks of age, when the final decision is made. The unwanted stock is then usually given away as pets.

Obviously, any newcomer to the Fancy who elects to keep more than one variety will require a great number of cages – and the space to keep them in (not to mention the money to feed the hordes!).

SELECTING VARIETIES

The selection of a particular variety with which to start should be given much consideration. Several trips to shows will prove invaluable in this respect. Look at all of the different colours and coat types on the showing bench and decide which ones you like. Next, talk to fanciers who have bred those particular varieties for several years and get them to tell you *all* of the pros and cons of the varieties. They will include:

a) Do they need regular bathing and/or grooming?
b) Do they breed true?
c) Can they be bred together? (Some varieties produce unacceptable progeny if bred together – see p.90.)
d) Will other varieties have to be kept in order to keep the colour and markings up to standard?

The beginner is well advised to start with one of the 'old standards' such as the dark golden, the black-eyed cream or the dark-eared albino. All of these breed true, will not produce any malformed young, and are hardy.

PURCHASING STOCK

Without doubt, anyone planning to purchase potential breeding and/ or exhibition stock should always go to a recognized and established breeder. True, some people have been lucky enough to purchase good stock from the local pet shop. I have even heard of the odd breeder who has won Best in Show with such stock, *but* this is the exception rather than the rule and, if you are intending to have a long and successful involvement with hamsters and the Hamster Fancy, you cannot afford to take such a risk.

By joining the relevant hamster club(s), you will be able to obtain details of all local breeders in your area. Some clubs will even supply you with full details as to the varieties in which these breeders specialize. Another good indication of the success of particular studs is to study the results of recent shows. These results and a detailed judge's report are published regularly in the specialized press. However, it should be borne in mind that it is possible for people to win an occasional show without having a good stock of hamsters, i.e. they may simply have been lucky in a single purchase.

The breeders that you should be looking for are the ones who have had *consistent* success over a period of at least 12–18 months. This will indicate that the persons concerned have been breeding their own stock and have therefore established a good line or lines.

Once you have identified a couple of potential suppliers of top-quality stock, you must contact them and discuss your requirements *prior to any visit*. All good hamster breeders will be only too pleased to discuss these with you, provided that you do not try to make out that you know everything. On the contrary, you should be quite open regarding your lack of expert knowledge on the subject, while not hiding your enthusiasm. Everyone likes to be flattered, provided that this is done in a not too flamboyant way. Treat a breeder well and you will be repaid in encouragement and guidance.

While it is true that no real fancier will risk his hard-earned reputation, often built up over ten or more years, by supplying inferior-quality stock, few are likely to give their *best* stock to a completely unknown person. Get to know the people concerned, treat them with the respect which they deserve, and breeders will be more inclined to give you stock that they would otherwise keep for themselves.

When you think that you have finally made contact with a supplier of suitable stock, arrange to visit the breeder and his hamstery *without agreeing to buy any stock*. This is simply a reconnaissance mission, where you will be looking at the breeder's current stock and the way in which it is kept. Only when you are 100 per cent happy that you have chosen the correct supplier should you make your order for stock. It is highly unlikely that this stock will be available at the time, and you will probably have to place an advance order, which may take 2–3 months for the breeder to satisfy. This will give you time to ensure that all is ready at your hamstery and so guarantee that your new charges will lead a comfortable life (see Chapter 3, Housing).

An initial order should consist of a breeding trio, i.e. two females and one male. It is not necessary for all three to be unrelated, but neither should they all come from the same litter (see Chapter 6, Genetics). Two females from one litter and a male from the litter of a cousin will be a good selection. Failing this, many breeders will be quite willing to allow you to purchase a pair of females and have the use of one of their studs at a future date, or sell you females that have already been mated and are 'in kindle' (pregnant). The fee for stud service can take the form of money, the pick of the litter, a return favour from you when you are in a position to do so, or simply a 'thank you' and the goodwill that goes along with it.

Most breeders will be happy with the last two forms of payment. I would *never* recommend any breeder to allow another person to have the pick of the litter, since invariably the stud's owner wants the same pup that the dam's owner wants! This can lead to great problems. Whatever you agree to, ensure that the deal is clearly understood *before* the mating takes place.

Do not rush to purchase stock. Take your time and look around at what is on offer. Many breeders who cannot themselves help you will still be happy to put you in touch with someone who can – and they may even be willing to help you choose the most likely candidates in a litter. However, it must always be borne in mind that *no one* can ever guarantee that any particular hamster will grow up to be a Best in Show winner. Nevertheless, an experienced exhibitor can help you to

Select young stock that is bright-eyed and inquisitive. This is best obtained from a top-quality breeder and exhibitor of several years' standing.

have a good chance of buying a potential winner! Ensure that, if you are intending to breed for exhibition, your purchases are all standard varieties (see Chapter 7, Exhibiting).

When you purchase your stock, ensure that you get the following information:

a) Date of birth,
b) Variety,
c) A 'pedigree' giving details of parentage for at least the last three generations.

This pedigree is not always in the same form as that for a dog, although forms intended for pedigree dogs will more than suffice. On p.36 is my own form for the pedigree that I give with every hamster that I sell. If you make your own, you can also use the blanks to take down the information regarding any hamsters that you buy.

RECORD-KEEPING

It is imperative, if you are to be successful in your hamstering career, that you maintain complete and accurate records of all of your hamsters from day one. These records should be kept on a card affixed to each cage, and also in a book or some other central information store (see Chapter 10, New Technology, for details of other record-keeping devices and methods). The record should contain the following information:

a) Variety,
b) Name and/or reference number,
c) Breeder, if applicable,
d) Date of birth,
e) Great-grandparents, grandparents and parents,
f) Siblings,
g) Breeding/mating details (including sizes of litters).

By attaching different-coloured cards to the cages, according to the variety, you will be able to see at a glance which variety is in a cage. All writing on these cards should be done using an indelible (waterproof) pen, since other inks will run when damp or when water is spilled on them, and this is almost guaranteed to happen in each and every hamstery at some time. Never use pencil, as the writing will fade and you will lose all the information. Never trust to memory either, as it can fail all too often.

Not all of the above details need be written on the card on the hamster's cage, but all (and more) should be recorded in the stud book, a central record (not necessarily a book) of all details pertaining

---

Colour and Markings ....
Coat Type ....
Sex ....
Date of Birth ....
Siblings; M .... F ....

McKamstery
Pedigree Certificate

Name of Hamster ....

Reg. No ....
Breeder ....
Owner ....
Address ....

AWARDS

	PARENTS	GRANDPARENTS	GREAT GRANDPARENTS	**AWARDS**
	SIRE Name Reg No Colour & Markings Coat Type Date of Birth Name and Address of Owner/Breeder	Sire Name Reg No Colour & Markings Coat Type Date of Birth	Sire Name Reg No Colour & Markings Coat Type Dam Name Reg No Colour & Markings Coat Type	
		Dam Name Reg No Colour & Markings Coat Type Date of Birth	Sire Name Reg No Colour & Markings Coat Type Dam Name Reg No Colour & Markings Coat Type	
	DAM Name Reg No Colour & Markings Coat Type Date of Birth Name and Address of Owner/Breeder	Sire Name Reg No Colour & Markings Coat Type Date of Birth	Sire Name Reg No Colour & Markings Coat Type Dam Name Reg No Colour & Markings Coat Type	
		Dam Name Reg No Colour & Markings Coat Type Date of Birth	Sire Name Reg No Colour & Markings Coat Type Dam Name Reg No Colour & Markings Coat Type	

I hereby certify the information on this Pedigree Certificate to be correct to the best of my knowledge.

Signed .... Date ....

An example of a pedigree form layout

to your hamsters. Without such a record, you will never be able to breed your hamsters successfully in an ordered and efficient manner. Neither will you be able to perpetuate a mutant colour, thereby risking the loss of it for ever.

It is a matter of convention that all males are assigned letters of the alphabet for recording purposes, while females are given numbers. This is due to the fact that, on average, a hamstery will consist of several times more female hamsters than males – at any one time and throughout the life of the hamstery. Some breeders combine these codes to identify any litters produced from a mating. For instance, if hamster A (male) is mated with hamster 1 (female), and this mating produces a litter of two females and one male, the females will be coded 1A1 and 1A2, and the male A1A. I find this method too complicated and fussy to maintain. Instead, I simply number all my males from 1 to infinity, and the females A to Z; when I get to the end of the alphabet for the first time, I start again, prefixing all letters with the first letter of the alphabet, e.g. AA, AB, AC, AD etc. When I get to the end of the alphabet for the second time, I prefix the letter with the second letter in the alphabet, e.g. BA, BB, BC, BD etc. When I come to the end of the alphabet for the 26th time(!), I prefix the letter with two As, e.g. AAA, AAB, AAC, AAD etc.

THE STUD BOOK

Many breeders use a loose-leaf folder for their stud book and are quite happy with this arrangement. However, when using such books, it is very easy for a page to be lost, either because it falls out or simply because you forget to replace it after removing it to copy the information. A hard-backed note book of A4 size is ideal and you will have no trouble with pages going missing. Enter the details of the females at one end of the book and those of the males at the other end, or have a separate book for each gender.

The layout of a typical page in a stud book

Name	*Reference*
Variety	
Date of birth	
Breeder	
Parents	
Paternal g. parents	Maternal g. parents
Paternal g.g. parents	Maternal g.g. parents
Notes (siblings etc.)	
Mating and breeding record and details	

SEXING HAMSTERS

Hamsters are easily sexed at an early age. The basic differences are the same as in most mammals, i.e. in the female the anal and vaginal openings are close together with no fur between them while, in the male, the anal and penal openings are further apart and there is fur on the area between the two openings. The male's testicles are not usually visible, other than a slight bulge under the skin in the area of the genitals.

In adult hamsters, the male is smaller than the female and has a more slender body than the female's rounded figure. The rear of the female is also rounded, while that of the male is elongated by his testes. This difference will not be as obvious in young animals, nor during cold weather. In such conditions, the testes are carried inside the male's body, in order to maintain them at a reasonable temperature. They can, however, still be seen from the underside of the hamster.

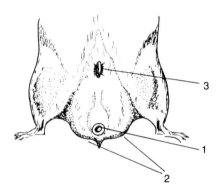

Fig. 3 Sexing a male hamster: **1.** Anal opening. **2.** Testicles. **3.** Penal opening.

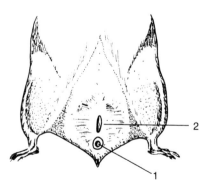

Fig. 4 Sexing a female hamster: **1.** Anal opening. **2.** Vaginal opening.

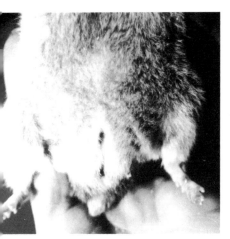 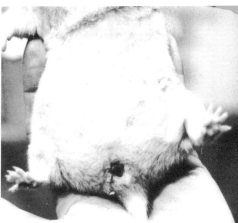

Left Sexual characteristics of a male hamster. The openings are some distance apart and have hair between them. The testicles can be seen as two bulges near the tail.
Right Sexual characteristics of a female hamster. The openings are close together, and the back end is rounded.

In order to view the genitalia of a hamster, it is necessary to invert the animal. In young hamsters, this can simply be done by holding the animal by the scruff of the neck and turning it over (p.45). In older animals, it is far easier to use the type of board favoured by experienced judges (p.143). This is simply a grid of wire or wire netting, shaped and sized to allow it to be used for scooping out a hamster from a standard show pen. (More details of this device and some of its many uses may be found in Chapter 8, Judging.)

Another method is simply to pick up the hamster by placing the hand over the animal with your fingers pointing towards its rear. The thumb and little finger are then brought together under the hamster in the region of its forelegs. The hamster can now be picked up and turned over. It should be noted that, as this is a completely unnatural position for the hamster, it will not be happy held in this way for a long period. Obviously, it is better to carry out the sexing quickly. With experience, this can be done in a matter of a few seconds, although I know of fanciers of several years' standing who have trouble in this area. If you cannot learn to sex hamsters accurately, then you will have great difficulty with the future breeding of your hamsters, while your juding will *never* be acceptable!

Remember the adage that 'practice makes perfect'; ask for help from an experienced breeder and get him to allow you to go through whole litters of hamsters to gain experience. It is, of course, essential that the

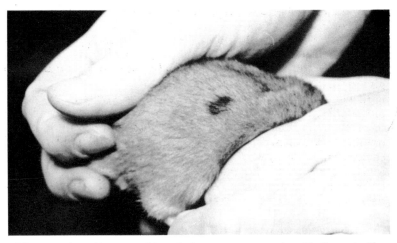

All hamsters have hip spots, although they are more prominent in the male. They are *not* a sign of illness.

experienced breeder is with you to tell you whether you are getting things right or not.

Female hamsters have twin rows of teats on their stomachs but so, too, do some males, and so these should not be used as an indication of the hamster's sex. Some books also refer to the hamster's hip spots as another sure indication of sex. Despite what these books say, hip spots (scent glands) are possessed by *both* sexes of hamster and are therefore no indication at all as to the animal's gender. Many people still mistake these scent glands for sores, especially during warm weather when the hamster has been licking them and the pink skin shows through clearly, thus emphasizing the gland itself. They are used to mark out the hamster's territory, in much the same way that a dog will use its urine.

AGE OF STOCK

The age at which you should buy your stock is another important consideration. Many breeders start by buying pups of 6–8 weeks of age. This is the absolute minimum age that you should consider buying stock, even though some breeders will sell pups as young as 4 weeks old. Hamsters will change dramatically between these ages and so you are merely hedging your bets by choosing older animals.

However, as hamsters have only a short life (24–36 months) and are capable of becoming pregnant as young as 6 weeks of age, hamsters above the age of 10–12 weeks are the oldest that you should normally buy. The only exceptions to these rules are when you specifically require stock from which you can breed almost immediately. Stock less than 12 weeks old should not, as a rule, be bred from, as it will not have had the opportunity to develop fully and mature sufficiently to give the best start in life to its litters.

At almost every show, you will find hamsters of 6 or more months of age offered as 'free to good homes' or at a very low price. Avoid them! Breeders do not discard stock at such ages unless they have one or more faults. These faults may be obvious to the gaze (non-standard colours, injuries etc.), or may manifest themselves when the hamster is handled (intractibility, nervous disposition etc.). Some may simply be infertile. Whichever is the case, they will prove to be more trouble than they are worth, unless, of course, all you require is a pet.

SIGNS OF ILLNESS

When you have finally made your decision as to which variety you wish to purchase and tracked down a suitable supplier, make arrangements to visit the hamstery to collect your stock. Remember to take along the cages (one for each hamster) or an equal number of suitable carrying boxes. These should contain shavings and bedding, plus some food – a piece of carrot, cabbage or such like. This will also serve to supply the hamsters with moisture on their trip to their new home. The amount of bedding in these cages should be altered to suit the prevailing ambient temperature, i.e. if it is very cold, supply a plentiful amount, whereas if it is very warm, only a minimal amount of bedding should be put in the cages. As the bedding also acts as a cushion against the knocks and bangs that the cage will undoubtedly receive on its way home, you should always include some, even in very warm weather.

Carefully examine each hamster offered to you, and reject any that have one or more of the following faults:

a) Diarrhoea,
b) Runny eyes,
c) Missing or damaged limbs and/or ears,
d) Scars,
e) Wounds,
f) Thin fur,
g) Bald patches,
h) Flaky skin.

As mentioned earlier, it is highly unlikely that an established breeder will try to sell you inferior stock, but it does not hurt to be prudent.

Hamsters will use their strong, sharp teeth to escape from a flimsy carrying box.

The plastic carrying boxes sold by pet shops are ideal for transporting newly purchased hamsters from the breeder's premises to your own hamstery. Remember to take at least one such carrier for every hamster that you intend to purchase.

TAKING YOUR STOCK HOME

Once you have selected your stock and paid and thanked the breeder, you should take your new charges back home and place them in the hamstery. Do not be tempted to handle them too much at this stage, but neither should you leave them entirely on their own. Remember that they have just been removed from a cosy nest, where they had the constant company and attention of their mother and siblings. It is a traumatic time for young animals.

If you have purchased hamsters (of the same sex) from the same litter, two of these can safely be kept together, at least for a few days, and maybe even for a week or two. In fact, my experience is that hamsters kept in this way for another 4–5 weeks will prosper much better than hamsters kept in individual cages from 6 weeks of age. Regular checks must be made on hamsters kept like this and, at the first signs of fighting, they must be placed in separate cages.

Speaking softly to the young animals will help to ease their stress, while a good selection of suitable food (see Chapter 4, Feeding) will also help to take their minds off their loneliness. A radio playing soothing music at a low volume will also help the animals during their first few days in their new environment, but don't leave it playing heavy metal music at full volume!

The day after their arrival, you must begin accustoming the pups to being handled although, if you have followed my recommendations and purchased your stock from a good breeder, he will almost certainly have been handling them for several weeks prior to your receiving them.

Before picking them up, allow the hamsters to smell your fingers, but do not poke them under the hamsters' noses. Hamsters are extremely short-sighted, and may mistake your fingers for food. Not being able to see them properly, and not yet recognizing your scent, a hamster will taste them!

On your first attempt to pick up the hamsters, use both hands in the form of a scoop. Do not lift them more than a few centimetres from the floor of the cage, thus allowing them to jump from your hands in safety if they so wish. If the hamster is content to stay in the palm of one hand for a time, slowly and gently stroke it with the fingers of your other hand. While doing this, keep up a constant low chatter, which will help put the hamster at ease and also set up a kind of rapport, whereby it will eventually recognize your voice as well as your scent.

Once your hamster is used to being picked up, you can use a better method of lifting it. Bring your hand forward, over the back of the hamster, with your fingers pointing towards the tail of the animal. Your thumb and little finger should be opened and then, as the hamster is under the palm of your hand, the thumb and little finger are closed around its body, behind its front legs. This is the best method of picking up a tame hamster.

A hamster which is obviously not tame, can be picked up using a piece of board (or a judging board) as a scoop, or using the loose skin at the back of the hamster's neck. If the skin is held correctly, a small nerve will be trapped and even the wildest hamster will become quite docile. This is exactly the way that the mother will pick up her babies, and nature supplied the 'nerve trick' in order to ensure that she could move the babies quickly and efficiently in times of danger, in order that all the family would have a better chance of survival.

There are several rules to consider when handling your hamsters. Do not make any sudden moves or noises. Do not squeeze the hamster. Do not try lifting the hamster high while balancing it on one hand. *Never* poke any hamster (no matter how tame you think it is) while it is still asleep or sleepy – hamsters feel the same about an alarm clock as do most human beings!

Taming is essential for several reasons:

a) Handling untamed animals causes them stress (the single biggest killer of captive animals),

b) Hamsters which cannot be easily handled on the show bench will lose points or even be disqualified,

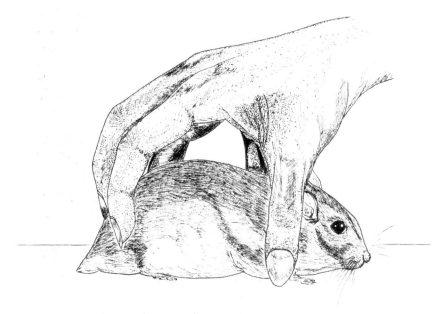

Fig. 5 Picking up a hamster. The fingers scoop up the animal, while the thumb and little finger secure it around the stomach. After picking up in this fashion, the hamster should be transferred to the palm of your other hand.

c) No one likes to handle any animal that they fear may bite them; consequently, untamed animals are not handled often enough, leading to neglect.

If you do not have the time and patience to ensure that all your animals are handled regularly and generally well looked after, you should not have any animals in your care.

Once you have acquired your stock and fully equipped your hamstery, as detailed in the next chapter, you will be ready to begin thinking about breeding your hamsters and, ultimately, developing a winning line. Do not, however, be tempted to run before you can walk. Take your time; discuss hamsters with other breeders and exhibitors, many of whom will have had many years of experience in the Fancy. Attend as many shows as possible, and not just those run by your local club. Each club and, to a large extent each judge, will have their own ideas on the 'perfect hamster', and only by seeking these ideas, and listening while keeping an open mind, will you learn and so form your own opinions.

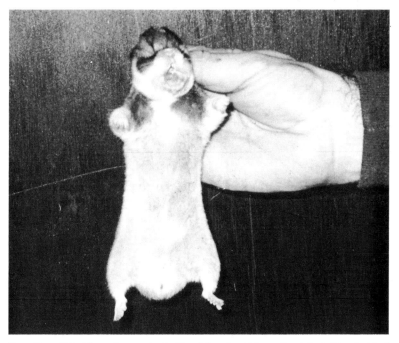

Even the wildest hamster can be held safely using this method. By taking hold of the excess skin at the back of the hamster's neck, the animal will be immobilized. Although this method does not hurt the hamster, and so is not cruel, it should only be used to pick up untamed hamsters, and should not be used as a matter of course.

CHAPTER 3

Housing

In the original *Hamster Handbook* of 1956, the authors stated a golden rule for hamsters: *'one hamster to one cage'*. This still holds true today, despite the fact that some breeders will tell you that they do occasionally get hamsters that will live happily with another hamster, usually a sibling. These are the exception, and it must always be remembered that hamsters kept together will almost invariably fight, causing damage to, if not killing, each other. It is just not worth the risk.

Before buying any hamsters, it will be necessary to ensure that you have sufficient cages for them. Although initially this number can simply be equal to the number of hamsters that you will purchase to begin your venture, it should be obvious that you will soon wish to breed from these animals, and so you will need spare cages for all of those future inhabitants. If you start with a breeding trio, you will need the following:

a) Three cages for existing stock,
b) One mating cage (p.73),
c) A *minimum* of two spare cages (one each for males and females) for each of the females, to house the litters.

If you then intend to keep any of the progeny of these matings (a necessity if you intend to establish a hamstery worthy of the name), then you will need one cage for each of the hamsters that you intend keeping. Such cages must be obtained well in advance, in order to ensure that hamsters are not kept in unsatisfactory accommodation while you set about buying or building their future homes. When any animal is kept in conditions which are not ideal, it endures stress which can lead to ill health for the animal, or become a contributory factor to its death. In any case, not to supply an animal with the basic requirements for a happy and healthy life is cruel.

I strongly recommend that anyone taking the Hamster Fancy seriously, and therefore intending to succeed in it, should possess a *minimum* of ten cages for each variety that it is intended to breed. While I know of many fanciers who have started their hamstering career with less than this number, almost all have very soon realized that they needed to obtain more. It is no use making this discovery when you have several cages full of young hamsters, all intent on picking a fight with each other. Not only is this foolishness, it is also cruel.

THE HAMSTERY

The room or building where hamsters are kept is known as a 'hamstery'. While it is possible to keep your hamsters dotted around your home, this is far from satisfactory, especially if you have ten or more cages! Decide *before* you buy your hamsters exactly where you are going to keep them and/or set up your hamstery.

A spare room in the house is often utilized, especially by those who live in apartments or houses without large gardens. While this idea works, without doubt the best situation is to have the hamstery in a hut or out-building that is quite separate from the human home, but still within easy reach. Having a hamstery more than a few minutes from one's own door may not seem too bad in the summer, or when you have a lot of spare time. In winter, however, having to travel a distance to carry out routine maintenance (feeding, watering and cleaning) leads to the whole process becoming a chore, and you will be less inclined to spend the time with your charges that you know you should. I therefore strongly recommend that, if you are serious about your hobby, you should utilize an existing out-house or invest in a garden shed or hut.

Some fanciers use a garage for their hamstery. While this in itself is perfectly acceptable, care should be taken not to have a car engine running for any length of time in the garage, as the resultant carbon monoxide gas produced will harm, or even kill, the hamsters in the garage. It is far better to have a hamstery in a building used solely for hamstering and, as previously mentioned, a garden hut is ideal.

The building

The hut should be at least 2m × 2m (2yd × 2yd) in area but larger if possible, with a door in one end, and windows down one side. A flat roof offers advantages over the standard pitched type, as the apex in the latter is simply a waste of space, but either type will suffice.

Ideally, the windows in the building should not face either south or southwest, as this would lead to the inmates being subjected to the full heat of the sun on a summer's day. The windows will cause a 'greenhouse effect' and this could lead to a high number of fatalities among your hamsters, due to heat stroke. Moreover, in the U.K., during the winter, or bad weather, south and southwesterly facing windows will bear the full brunt of the prevailing winds, which will

A wooden hut suitable for a hamstery. By placing it in the shade and shelter of a couple of trees, temperature control will be easier.

not only cause draughts and chill the hamstery, but will also drive in the rain through the gaps around these windows. A quiet, shaded area at the bottom of the garden is ideal; trees and hedges can be used to give shelter to the hamstery.

The hamstery needs to be well insulated in order to maintain a fairly even temperature throughout the year. Assuming that you intend to follow my recommendations and use an out-building or hut, you should line the whole building, including the floor, with polystyrene tiles or sheets of at least 25mm (1in) thickness. It is important that the floor of the building is treated in this way as well as the sides and roof, because cold strikes up from the ground and, as we intend to keep the temperature of the building as even as possible, this is one area that must not be neglected. The polystyrene on the walls and roof must be protected by a covering of hardboard or, even better, 6mm (¼in) marine-quality plywood. This should be thicker (12mm or ½in minimum) on the floor of the building. Insulation will ensure that your stock is kept in adequate and comfortable conditions, but it will also help you, because you will not find it so much of a chore in cold weather to stay in the hamstery to feed or handle your animals, thus ensuring that you will get more pleasure and enjoyment out of your chosen hobby. Good insulation will also reduce the amount of energy necessary to heat the hamstery during cold weather, reducing heating bills dramatically.

Ensure that all windows and doors are well fitting and fit draught-excluders for safety's sake. Windows are best if double-glazed, although it is unlikely that you will have proper double-glazed units in a garden shed! This can be rectified in several ways. Separate frames of glass can be fixed over the existing frames; this need not prevent the windows being opened, provided that care is taken and thought given to the problem. (Polythene sheeting can be tacked over the whole area of the windows, but this also makes opening the windows difficult.) I use frames covered with clear polycarbonate sheeting such as is used in the manufacture of vandal-proof bus shelters.

These frames are constructed and fitted in such a way as to allow the windows to be opened and/or the ventilators to function. It is worth bearing in mind that the insulation is intended to function all year round, keeping out both excessive heat and excessive cold. Fresh air is still, of course, essential for the health and well-being of the hamstery's inmates, and so adequate and controllable ventilation must also be incorporated into the design. This is best achieved by fitting adjustable air vents in the door, at the opposite end of the building and in at least one window. At least one of the windows must be capable of being fully opened, with a wire-mesh frame fitting over the opening to keep out cats, wild birds and other animals. A similar frame is also needed for the doorway. This is important because, when there is a hot spell, temperatures in buildings can soar. Even with adequate ventilation, as described here, temperatures in my hamstery have reached about 25°C (77°F). Without such ventilation, it would probably have reached 35°C (95°F) or higher, killing most (if not all) of the animals inside. The wire door will also help to keep out unwanted human visitors who, seeing a completely open building, may just fall victim to temptation and 'have a nosy', with all of the possible dangers which that entails.

Although not a panacea, curtains or blinds will help to limit the amount of sunlight allowed into your hamstery and thus help regulate the temperature.

Electricity is needed for the hamstery, both to supply light and heat and also to provide the means of powering a refrigerator and any tools that you may wish to use to service the cages and/or hamstery. All electricity supplies must be installed in a safe and competent manner. Unless you are experienced in this type of work, and fully conversant with all the safety requirements, pay a qualified electrician to do the work. Get an expert to advise you on this matter. As a minimum, you will need lighting – both on demand (i.e. at the flick of a switch) and timed (see p.50); a socket for the heating; a socket for the refrigerator (if fitted); and a spare pair of sockets for tools etc.

Security

There will always be someone who will wish to deprive others of possessions, be they jewels, a stereo or even hamsters. Some people also seem to get a perverse pleasure from damaging property and injuring animals and human beings. You must, therefore, ensure that the hamstery is protected from the unwanted attentions of such people. The first step towards this is the fitting of a good-quality lock.

This lock can be a top-quality padlock, fitted on a suitable hasp and staple, or a five-lever mortise lock. Do not rely on the lock fitted to the shed as standard by the manufacturer. On the whole, these locks are of very poor construction and are not really worthy of the name; they are fitted merely to keep the door closed, rather than as a form of security. All hasps and staples should be bolted, rather than screwed, to the building, and the hasp must be of the type whereby, when the lock is in position, it is impossible for anyone to tamper with the bolts. As an added precaution, the nuts can be brazed (welded) on to the bolts on the inside of the shed walls. A cover, made from an old rubber inner tube and placed over the padlock, will prevent the ingress of dirt and water, thereby lengthening the active life of the lock. Treat all locks and hinges with a good-quality oil at regular intervals, as this will also lengthen their working life, saving you the trouble and expense of replacing them.

Windows, too, must be provided with locks and, if you intend to leave them open during warm weather, the covering frames must be secured in position to keep out unwanted visitors. Burglar alarms can also be fitted, and these are covered in Chapter 10, New Technology.

Ensure that you have at least one spare key for every lock that you use, in case the original is lost. This is particularly important when the lock is one of the self-locking types (i.e. it is not necessary to use a key to fasten the lock). With such locks, it is very easy to secure the door, only to discover that you have left the key inside the building!

Lighting

A good strong light must be fitted to enable you to work in the hamstery during the dark evenings of the winter. This should be a standard 100 or 150W bulb; if your hamstery is large, you may find it more satisfactory to have two bulbs (one at each end of the hamstery) in order to avoid dark areas, or standing in your own light. Do *not* fit a fluorescent light; such lights have been known to cause fits in hamsters and also to cause the mothers to scatter their litters, due to the strobe effect which they produce.

You will also require a time-switch-operated light, if you intend to breed your stock all year round, as a hamster's oestrus cycle is dependent upon the ratio of daylight to darkness (photoperiodism). By fixing a small (60 or 100W) bulb to operate and supplement the daylight, hamsters can be fooled into believing that it is constantly summer. Heat, although useful for comfort and other reasons, plays little part in this (see Chapter 5, Breeding).

The ideal is to give the hamsters 18 hours of daylight in every 24-hour period or, as a minimum, 14 hours of light to 10 hours of darkness. By carefully thinking this through, it is possible to arrange the 'day' to finish about 30–45 minutes before your normal time to visit the hut and feed the hamsters. As this is the time when most female hamsters tend to come into heat, it will make life much easier and more convenient for you. If it is convenient for you to visit and work in the hamstery at, say, 9.00pm, you should set the time-switch-operated light to go out at about 8.15–8.30pm. During the winter, this will mean that the light should be set to operate from about 2.00am, until about 8.30am (when it is light). It will then need to be set to switch the light on again at about 3.30–4.00pm, when darkness falls again.

You will also find it useful to have an adjustable reading lamp in the hamstery. If this is fitted with a 'daylight bulb', you will be able to judge the real colours of your stock. These bulbs are rather expensive, but well worth the investment. Readily available from any good photographic store, they are essential to every serious hamster breeder, even when the natural light appears to be quite good. It is worth noting that most experienced judges of exhibition hamsters always use such a light on the show bench, and many clubs now insist that every judge uses such a light whenever possible.

Heating

Heaters used for the hamstery need to be carefully selected and should be thermostatically controlled. The ideal year-round temperature in the hamstery should be between 18° and 20°C (64° and 68°F).

To reduce the risk of fire, no flames must be present, and so this precludes the use of paraffin- or other similar heaters. These heaters are also unsuitable due to the dangerous fumes that they inevitably emit. In the home, the chances are that the room will have a central-heating radiator fitted, but this will not usually apply to an outbuilding or shed. Radiant electric fires are totally unsuitable in the hamstery, because the risk of fire is too great. Some breeders use the tubular heaters designed for use in greenhouses, but I find that, unless they are extremely large (or you use several of them), they do no more than keep the chill off the air (just!). Oil-filled electric storage heaters are quite useful and may be run using cheaper off-peak electricity.

My own hamstery is heated by two 1kW electric fan heaters, each operated via a thermostat. By using two, I ensure that the temperature will not drop dramatically if one heater fails. I also wire in a small

(15W) light bulb in such a way that it will only work if the heater is functioning correctly. This gives me a visual check on the heaters' operation. The heaters are placed high in the hamstery, where shavings, bedding and other such debris cannot fall on them (which could be a fire risk). They are also placed as far apart as possible, in order to spread their heating effect around the hamstery. Care must also be taken to ensure that the heater is positioned so as not to direct the stream of warmed air directly at the hamsters' cages, since this can make life very uncomfortable for the inmates.

The thermostats used for controlling the heaters must be rated to carry the high current that the heaters will need (about 10amp each). If in doubt, check with a properly qualified and experienced electrician, whose advice should also be sought as to their fitting, wiring etc.

Large radiant-heat bulbs, suspended from the roof, can also be used. If you do decide to use these, ensure that there is no danger of visitors (or even yourself) walking into them, i.e. attach them well above head height. This will be impossible in many rooms and huts. In these situations, the bulbs can sometimes be fixed on to a wall, but once again ensure that they will not be in a position to cause accidents or fires. A frame of wire mesh around these bulbs will help prevent accidents, but ensure that the frame is easy to remove, to facilitate service and replacement of bulbs.

Precautionary measures

Smoking

Smoking in the hamstery must not be allowed, both because of the obvious fire risk, and also for the (less obvious) risk to the health of the hamsters. Even if you smoke yourself, it is worth imposing this no smoking rule for everyone – including yourself!

Escapes

Hamsters are born escapologists and will get out of their cages at the first opportunity. No matter how careful you are, you are bound to have several hamster escapes during your hamstering career. You should try to limit these by ensuring that all cages have a good fastening – and that it is always used!

To recapture escapees, there are several methods that you can employ. The first is to use a pile of books, stacked so that they represent a set of steps. This stairway leads to the lip of a bucket (or similar), at the bottom of which is a pile of food, including some item which has a strong aroma, such as a hard-boiled egg. The whole trap should be set up near to the place from which the hamster escaped, or close to the area in which it is thought to be hiding, and left overnight.

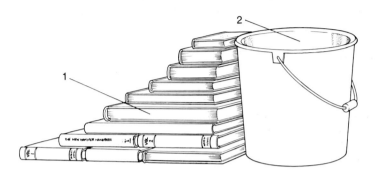

Fig. 6 Book trap. This trap can be easily made, and should be set up in the area in which the errant hamster has escaped. **1.** Stepped books with food trail. **2.** Bucket containing strong-smelling food (e.g. cabbage).

All things being equal, the errant rodent will be found in the bottom of the bucket the next morning, having fallen in while trying to reach the food (hamsters having an insatiable appetite and desire to fill their food store). The smooth, sheer sides of the bucket will ensure that it will not be able to climb out. Over the years, I have found that this method works very well.

If you wish to be a little more creative, you may want to make your own trap, on the lines of that shown on the next page.

The dimensions are not crucial, as long as you ensure that the opening is large enough to allow a good-sized hamster to pass through comfortably. The body of the cage should be long enough to allow the whole of the hamster through the door before he trips the wire, closing the door. Experiment with the catch to ensure that it really will work *every* time. There is little which is more frustrating than finding a trap that has been emptied of bait, but has not caught the escapee.

It is possible to buy ready-made 'live-trap' cages, but almost all of these are intended to capture mice, and so are too small for adult hamsters. Of these, probably the most well-known and, to my mind, the best, is the Longworth trap. This is made from solid, thick aluminium and consists of a small detachable tunnel leading to the 'nest box'. At the nest-box end of the tunnel is a trip lever which, when activated by the hamster, will cause the door at the opening of the tunnel to close. An automatic catch then locks the door, thus preventing the trapped hamster from escaping. A small amount of both food and bedding must be placed in the nest box before setting;

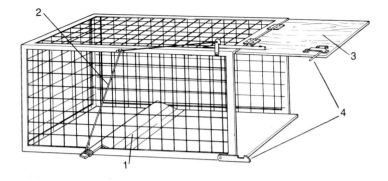

Fig. 7 Home-made hamster trap. A trap of this nature will enable escaped hamsters to be caught safely. At least one of these traps should be permanently set and baited with food in every hamstery to catch any escapees. **1.** Trip. **2.** Wire for release. **3.** Hinged door. **4.** Catch (to secure door after hamster has sprung the trap).

again a small amount of hard-boiled egg is ideal to attract the hamster into the trap.

Any trap that you set *must* be inspected every few hours or, at the very least every morning and evening, in order to ensure that no animal is left in stressful conditions for longer than is necessary.

Wild rodents

As mentioned earlier, there will always be a possibility of wild rodents finding their way into the hamstery. It is unwise to set any kind of trap that is designed to kill these mice, or to lay any poison, as there is the obvious danger that one of your hamsters may be injured if it escapes from its cage. Use one of the proprietary live-traps, available from most pet stores, or a Longworth trap. At least one of these should be permanently set in your hamstery and checked at least twice daily.

Any trap which catches a wild rodent must be thoroughly disinfected before re-use, to minimize the possibility of transmitting diseases from the wild animal to your stock.

If you do catch a mouse in one of these traps, either it should be killed humanely or, if you do not wish to take its life, the trap should be left fastened while you transport it to an area at least 1000m (1000yd) from anybody's home, where it can be released. To release a mouse closer to a home than this is asking for a second visit.

Two commercially available 'live-traps' suitable for hamsters. The rear trap is known as a Longworth trap.

A hamster caught in a plastic 'field-trap' available from pet shops.

Flying insects

Flies and other such pests will become a nuisance in warm weather, regardless of how clean you keep your hamsters' cages and the hamstery itself. Do not spray any fly-killer in the hamstery while it contains any animals or any foods. This means that, if you do decide to spray, you must empty the whole hamstery – clearly impractical. It should be noted, however, that there are now some sprays on the market which are intended for use in areas containing human food, and these may be used more safely than others. Always read the label well and, if in doubt, check with the manufacturer *before* use.

A better method, and one that is used by many fanciers, is to employ the old-fashioned fly-papers. These are available from most hardware stores and consist of long strips of paper coated with a sticky substance that contains an insecticide. They are perfectly safe for this type of use. They should be hung in a position where you and other visitors to your hamstery are unlikely to bump into them, as they are excellent at removing hair from a human head!

Shelving and storage

Obviously, all cages need to be on shelves of some sort, and so thought must be given to this at the initial stage. The design of hut that I have recommended lends itself to what has become an almost standard layout.

Shelves should begin at about 1m (1yd) from the floor, unless space is at a premium, in which case they can be as low as 300m (12in) from the floor. They should not be placed lower than this, because the cages that will be placed upon them will then be subjected to draughts. One disadvantage with low shelving is that, as one gets older, constantly bending down becomes more uncomfortable. The younger reader may dismiss this caution, thinking that it does not concern him, but old age comes to us all eventually! Another major disadvantage with shelving at a low level is that shavings, debris, spilled food and dirt will build up under the shelving, and this is almost impossible to clean up adequately.

The space between the shelves must be given careful consideration. Not only must there be sufficient space for the free circulation of air, but there must also be space for the water bottle that each cage will require. Even if you are using one of the more modern methods of delivering water to the cage's inhabitants (see Chapter 10, New Technology), you will still need to leave space. It is false economy to leave insufficient space between shelves, in the hope of cramming more cages into the total space available. All this will do is to make life difficult and, also, prevent the water from being delivered to the cage occupants efficiently.

The floor of the hamstery must be kept scrupulously clean, in order to maintain healthy conditions and discourage wild birds and animals from visiting the building. Once birds, mice and rats get to know that there is a regular supply of food on the floor of your hamstery, they will become almost impossible to keep at bay. Not only will they become a nuisance, but they will also spread disease. Covering the floor with linoleum or some other strong, waterproof covering will make life much easier.

To help you keep the hamstery clean, you will require a good stiff-bristled handbrush and dustpan (for the shelving), while a full-sized sweeping brush will be essential for keeping the floor clean and tidy.

Storage

If shelving starts at 1m (1yd) from the floor, the space underneath can be utilized for storage of food, shavings and bedding. All food and bedding must be stored in rodent-proof containers. As we are talking about quite large quantities, plastic dustbins will prove satisfactory, although some manufacturers now produce containers specifically for storing animal feeds. Whichever type you choose, the containers must be clearly marked with the contents and have a secure lid.

A smaller container should be utilized to store enough food to feed all of the hamsters in the hamstery every night. This will make life much easier for you; the container can be either a purpose-made food container or a large used tin or jar, such as those in which biscuits and coffee are packed. A suitably sized scoop should be included in this tin, thus ensuring that each cage receives the correct amount of food.

I use different styles of container for food and rubbish, since mistakes easily occur, especially when visitors are at the hamstery, or one's friends are looking after the animals while you are on holiday. For this reason, I do not use plastic dustbins, as people always assume that they are for the rubbish, regardless of any labels that may be attached. Instead, I use containers sold for the storage of dry dog foods; these are much stronger and have a far more secure lid than any plastic dustbin that I have found. For rubbish, I use a frame which holds a plastic refuse sack. This sack is changed regularly and *never* left for any time with any potentially smelly rubbish inside.

An incinerator is invaluable for the disposal of the waste bedding and shavings. In cases of infection in a hamstery, *all* bedding and shavings must always be burned, and this must be done as soon as the waste is taken from the cages, i.e. on cleaning day. Stored waste is a potential hazard, not to mention a producer of smells.

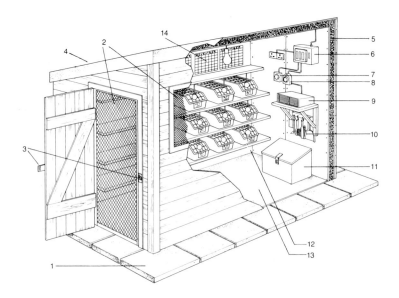

Fig. 8 1. Hamstery: 1. Solid base of paving slabs or concrete. Leave a space under the shed; this allows air to circulate, thereby helping to prevent the wooden floor and base from rotting. All timber, including the base and roof, must be well treated with top-quality wood preservative prior to the shed's erection.

2. Wire door and window covers. To allow adequate ventilation during hot periods, while excluding vermin and unauthorized human visitors. Ensure that the covers are capable of being locked into place, maintaining security at all times.

3. Security. A strong top-quality padlock affixed to a sturdy hasp and staple is essential, and the building must be kept locked at all times. Keep a spare key in a safe place, especially if using a 'self locking' padlock (i.e. one where it is not necessary to employ a key to lock it). The addition of a good alarm system is recommended, and is well worth the investment of both time and money.

4. Heavy-duty roofing felt, securely fixed. This must be regularly inspected, and repaired or replaced as and when necessary.

5. Insulation. All walls, the roof and the floor should be insulated with thick polystyrene sheets in order to keep the hamstery's temperature even throughout the year. A covering of plywood will ensure that the fragile polystyrene sheeting is not damaged.

6. Fuse box. All electrical work must be undertaken by someone competent in this field. In order to guard against fires, all fuses must be correctly rated. This applies both to the fuse box and the appliance itself.

7. Time switch to control one bulb in order to give a 16-hour day throughout the year. Do not use fluorescent lighting in the hamstery.

8. Thermostat to control fan-heater. This must be correctly rated to carry the heavy load of the heater. A temperature of about 15°C (59°F) is recommended in the hamstery.

9. Electric fan-heater, thermostatically controlled. This must be positioned where shavings and other such debris cannot fall on the elements, causing a fire risk. The inlet area should be cleaned on a regular basis.

10. Cleaning implements. To keep both the hamstery and the hamster cages neat and tidy.

11. Feed bin. Must be rodent-proof and clearly marked as 'Feed Only'. Use a different design for rubbish.

12. Shelving. To suit your design of cage. It should be secured to the wall or floor to prevent it accidentally toppling, but you must be able to clean under and behind the shelves in order to prevent the build-up of shavings, food etc.

13. Floor covering. Linoleum or some other waterproof and easily cleanable material will help facilitate cleaning, exclude draughts and prevent spillage from soaking into the wooden floor. Under this is a lining of polystyrene covered with top-quality plywood.

14. Wall charts and calendars. Handy to keep track of births, shows etc. A chalkboard is also a very useful addition to any hamstery.

All food, including titbits and food supplements must be kept in air-tight containers at all times.

Work surface

Under the window, a flat laminated table-top, should be provided. This will prove enormously useful for all kinds of purposes – handling stock in good 'natural' light (although an adjustable reading lamp with a 'daylight' bulb fitted will still prove beneficial), repairing cages, cleaning cages, writing notes, providing a base for the mating cage so that the mating may be properly supervised. A sink in the hamstery, with running water and proper drainage, will also prove extremely useful. This is, however, a luxury that most hamsteries will not possess, since it is difficult (and often impossible) to arrange suitable drainage for such a sink, even if it is fairly easy to supply running water. As large quantities of water will still be required, a large container – regularly cleaned and refilled – will be needed. The type of barrel sold for home-brewing is ideal. It is best to choose one made from coloured plastic, rather than semi-transparent material, as this will help prevent the growth and consequent build-up of algae in the water. A good-quality tap, which cannot be left turned on by mistake, should be fitted to this barrel.

Very few hamsteries will have a fully functioning sink with running water. A barrel such as this will save you many trips back to the kitchen to fill water bottles.

A couple of aquaria, either plastic or glass, should live permanently on this surface. They can be used as mating pens and/or holding pens for stock while cages are being cleaned or repaired, and each must have a secure wire covering. Under this table-top, I have installed a couple of cupboards. These provide excellent storage space for stud books, pens, record cards, judging frames, cleaning utensils, etc. Such cupboards can be bought quite cheaply at any of the many do-it-yourself stores that are close to every town and city, or may be purchased second-hand for even less money. Reasonably priced sinks can also be bought at such establishments. Remember that all work surfaces should be at a convenient height for comfort.

The addition of a small refrigerator to a hamstery will enable you to store fruit, vegetables and other perishable materials for longer periods, and I recommend this to every serious hamster breeder.

Construction of shelves

It is possible to purchase ready-made shelving in various forms. However, if you decide to do this, ensure that the spacing between the shelves is suitable for your choice of cages. If you choose the laboratory type of cage, you can also purchase racks of shelves specifically designed for these cages. They also have the advantage of being on wheels, which is a great boon when cleaning the hamstery floor. If your hamstery suits this type of set-up, I strongly recommend them.

If you are building your own shelving, you can use either timber or metal angles. While wood is easier to work with, it is liable to sag under the weight of the cages. Metal angle will not, but it will need drilling and bolting to fix it, although some metal angle can be purchased ready drilled along its length. Again, it is possible to build your own racks of shelves, and to fix wheels or castors on them for ease of cleaning. Any timber battens used should be at least 50mm × 25mm (2in × 1in) and all joints should be secured with screws and not nails.

Types of cages

Cages can be divided easily into four main types:

a) Home-made cages,
b) Commercial breeders' cages,
c) Pet cages,
d) Semi-made cages.

All hamster cages should be kept on suitable shelving and clearly marked with details of the inmate.

Home-made cages

These are usually made of wood, this being the easiest material for the amateur to work with. The *minimum* size for a hamster cage for a single hamster is 300mm × 300mm × 180mm high (12in × 12in × 7in high). For a cage for a breeding female, this size should be increased to 300mm × 400mm × 210mm high (12in × 16in × 8in high)

There are several designs that are suitable for the hamsters, but you first need to ascertain how you will keep the cages, i.e. on shelves, on racks, stacked on top of each other, on table-tops, etc. Once you have decided on this, you can then decide which of the following designs suits your needs. I recommend that, for cage-holding, you use racks which can be pulled away from the wall to allow cleaning behind them. Failing this, shelves (either open or solid) will do the trick, provided that you can still clean under them, thus preventing a build-up of shavings, bedding and food.

All wood used in the construction of hamster cages must be at least 12mm (½in) thick marine-quality plywood. Solid wood, some breeders argue, is better but its price is prohibitive. All surfaces of the cage must be painted with non-toxic paint. Two coats will suffice for the outside (gloss is best here), but three or four coats of an eggshell emulsion is recommended for the inside surfaces. Choose a light-coloured paint for the inside. Do not use white paint, as it is believed that constant exposure to white surroundings can cause stress

A home-made wooden cage, with an all-wire front which opens to allow easy access to the interior for ease of cleaning and maintenance.

problems (and thus ill health); light blue is to be recommended. All edges of the timber must fit snugly, as hamsters will gnaw at any point where they feel a draught. Covering exposed edges with metal strips or wire netting will help protect them, thus ensuring that the cage has a long and useful life.

All wire used should be of welded-mesh construction, and at least 18SWG. *Do not* use chicken mesh, as it is not strong enough to withstand the concerted attack of a hamster for very long, and so will need to be replaced at regular intervals. Chicken mesh will also require a frame on which it can be mounted, whereas welded mesh will not. Thus any saving in the cost of chicken mesh will soon be lost.

Every cage must have a good-quality fastener, as hamsters are born escapologists and will soon find their way out of an insecure cage.

Never use hamster cages with low sides, as the inmates will be constantly kicking out the sawdust, causing more mess for you to clean up. In breeding cages, low sides (particularly at the opening of the cage) can cause problems with young pups running out and falling and injuring themselves. At least one side of the cage must consist of wire netting, in order to allow the air to circulate freely. Failing this, a couple of suitable ventilators should be incorporated in the design of the cage.

Hamsters, being burrow dwellers in the wild state, feel secure in small tight spaces such as this commercially-made plastic nest box.

Every hamster cage needs to have provision for holding a record card. This can either be a purpose-made frame, a drawing pin into the wooden exterior of the cage or some other device. All writing on record cards should be carried out in indelible ink, otherwise, if the card gets damp, you may well lose all the information. A central stud book, containing *all* relevant information on your hamstering activities and the hamsters themselves should also be kept.

Hamsters do not need separate sleeping quarters, but many owners like to provide a nest box. If you are one of those people, then the nest box should measure about 150mm × 150mm × 150mm high (6in × 6in × 6in high) and have a hole about 50mm × 50mm (2in × 2in) in one side, for an entrance. In order to facilitate cleaning, the lid or one side of the nest box should be completely removable, or at the very least hinged to open fully. This nest box can be placed on the floor of the cage or, if height allows it, on a shelf about 50–60mm (2–2½in) from the floor of the cage.

Although some designs for home-made cages involve glass, this material requires careful handling, as it is all too easy to break it, with possible damage to yourself and/or the hamsters in the cages. If you feel it is essential to use some transparent material, use clear polycarbonate sheeting. Although almost unbreakable, this material will, in time, become scratched and require replacing.

BOX CAGE

This is, as the name suggests, simply a box with a netting lid on the top. In order to help air circulation, two small (25mm or 1in diameter) holes are drilled about 50mm (2in) from the bottom of the cage. These are then covered *on the inside* with wire netting or (even better) perforated tin, in order to prevent the hamster from gnawing at the hole, thus creating an escape route.

This design of cage has the advantage of preventing the inmate from rushing out when the cage is opened, but can only be cleaned out by completely inverting the cage. When this action is taken, the lid can become a real nuisance. This problem can, however, be overcome by making the lid completely removable, either by having it located on pins and then fastened, or by using pin hinges.

HALF–GLASS–FRONTED CAGE

By taking the last-mentioned design and modifying it, we come to a cage with more advantages and fewer disadvantages. The cage is constructed as before, but the lid is left solid and hinged at the back. The front of the cage is replaced by a sheet of 3mm (24oz) glass or polycarbonate sheeting to half of the height; this can be permanently fixed in place if desired, but can cause problems when cleaning the cage. It is far better to make this glass removable, and this can be easily achieved by using metal angle or runners available from any good

D.I.Y. store. Do not use such runners along the bottom of the cage, as they will quickly fill with wood shavings/sawdust. A metal handle with which to open the glass or polycarbonate can easily be crafted from metal or purchased.

The top half of the cage is covered by a door of netting. This can be built on a wooden or metal frame but, if you use strong welded–mesh netting as recommended earlier, this will be unnecessary. The lid and the wire door both require fasteners to secure them. The wire front will eliminate the need for ventilation holes, which were required in the former design, while the wire front means that these cages can be

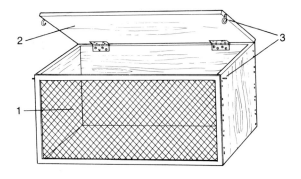

Fig. 9 Wire-fronted cage: **1.** Hinged wire-frame front. **2.** Hinged lid. **3.** Catches.

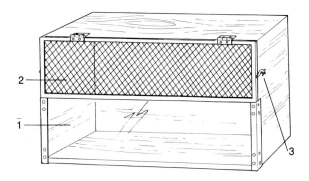

Fig. 10 Half-glass-fronted cage: **1.** Glass or clear polycarbonate sheeting. **2.** Hinged wire frame. **3.** Catches.

easily and safely stacked one on top of the other, and still allow the hamster breeder to see his charges and service the cage, without having to disturb it.

GLASS-FRONTED CAGE

Similiar to the last design, this style of cage has a front consisting of a single piece of 3mm (24oz) glass (or polycarbonate sheeting) which is completly removable. Coupled with a hinged or removable netting lid, this will help facilitate thorough cleaning.

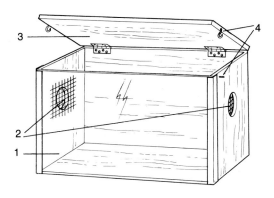

Fig. 11 Glass-fronted cage: **1.** Glass or clear polycarbonate sheeting. **2.** Ventilators. **3.** Hinged lid. **4.** Catches.

WIRE-FRONTED CAGE

Almost identical to the glass-fronted design, this cage has a solid lid and a wire front. Both should be hinged and/or completely removable for cleaning purposes.

PARLETT-TYPE CAGE

Designed by Bob Parlett, a very experienced fancier from the Midlands, this type of cage is extremely easy to make, and is used extensively by breeders all over the country.

It is possible to make this cage from one piece of wood, with only four cuts, as detailed in the illustration on the next page.

The front of the cage is made from welded mesh, secured with a wire fastener.

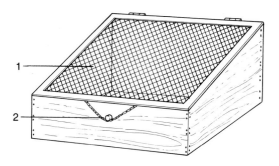

Fig. 12 Parlett-type cage: **1.** Hinged wire front. **2.** Catch.

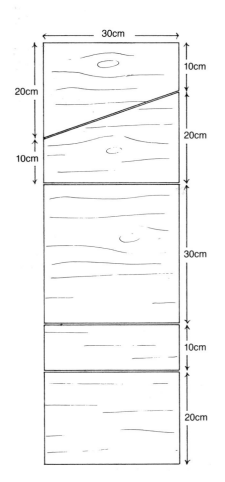

Fig. 13 Parlett-type cage construction. The measurements given are ideal for individual hamsters, particularly youngsters. Simply saw into desired shapes/sizes and then nail or screw timber together. 12mm (½in) exterior quality plywood is ideal, but it must be painted with non-toxic emulsion on the inside and gloss paint on the exterior.

A home-made Parlett-type wooden cage, which can be simply built from one piece of wood (see Fig.13). The front is best made from timber, rather than the wire used here, as this will reduce draughts and prevent the hamster from kicking out the shavings.

BREEDING CAGE

For breeding females, a larger cage will be needed. The design illustrated here has proved extremely practical over many years of use. It can be altered slightly to suit individual requirements and tastes (e.g. the lower front section can be made from wire; the cage can be made smaller for general hamster keeping, etc.). The side can either be

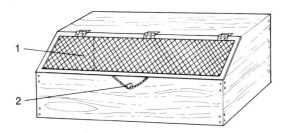

Fig. 14 Breeding cage: **1.** Hinged wire-frame front. **2.** Catch.

shaped or left square, while the wire front does not require a frame and the 'hinges' are simply wire staples. The Parlett-type design can also be made in a larger size for use as a breeding cage.

YOUNG STOCK CAGE

Young stock does not require such large cages, and so most breeders keep these animals in slightly smaller versions of their other cages. The Parlett cage, described earlier, is simplicity itself to make, and requires no woodworking knowledge, nor special tools. The timber is cut as indicated, and then the cage is screwed together, after which it is painted. The wire top is then fitted and the cage is ready for its new tenant. If you are making several of these cages at once, it is best to cut the timber pieces all at the same time, and then the wire tops. The construction then takes the form of a production line.

Commercial cages

People breed hamsters for many different reasons. Where that reason is financial (e.g. for sale of stock to the pet trade, medical research), off-the-shelf caging has been developed to cater for this demand. As far as hamsters are concerned, there are several designs of cage on offer. Before looking at them, we need to consider carefully the qualities that we will require from our cages.

All of the cages must be of a suitable size (in all dimensions) and be of a shape which will suit the hamster and the breeder. They must also be easy to clean and maintain (this includes feeding and the provision of water).

A commercial 'laboratory' cage, recommended for use in a hamstery.

Several companies manufacture cages that will be suitable for our purpose. All of these cages seem to have been developed for use in laboratories or similar institutions. They tend to be manufactured from a high-quality nylon-type of material, which can be cleaned at very high temperatures (for sterilization purposes). The bars of the cages are made from stainless steel. These features make the cages highly suitable for hamster breeding, although the price does tend to be rather high. However, I am a great believer in the old adage that 'you only get what you pay for', and these are top-quality cages which, if looked after, will last for many years. I have several which are over 10 years old and, during that time, they have been used almost continuously.

Pet cages

Almost every pet shop sells a wide variety of cages for pet hamsters. While most of these are quite suitable for the pet-keeper, very few are fit for our purposes, i.e. large-scale breeding. The better ones are those of box shape, with one end that opens for servicing of the cage. They have a hard plastic base, with sides about 30–40mm (1–1½in) high, and the rest of the cage is constructed from chromed bars. They are relatively cheap, and, if looked after well, will last for several years.

Semi-made cages

Most breeders have little time to spend building their cages from scratch, while many do not wish to spend the relatively large amounts of money on commercially available cages. These people choose to utilize various items that are easily and cheaply available and yet, with only a little effort can be transformed into usable cages.

One of the main items used for this purpose is the ubiquitous plastic washing-up bowl (although care must be taken to ensure that the bowl has square, i.e. not rounded, sides).

To turn these bowls into cages, it is only necessary to construct a good netting frame to slide over the top. This can be done in a matter of minutes, and at very little cost, either by building a wooden frame and then fitting the wire mesh on to it, or simply by folding the wire mesh so that it slides on. While these cages are not large enough for breeding females, they do make suitable cages for individual hamsters, especially youngsters.

Some breeders use old aquaria to house their hamsters. These are quite good for a single pet hamster, as they allow the occupant to be seen at all times. However, they are very difficult to clean, easy to break, offer poor insulation, are bulky and quite expensive. For these reasons, I do not recommend their use in the serious hamstery, except

Another method of turning a plastic bowl into a usable hamster cage. This type of cage is not, however, big enough for breeding females.

A hamster cage made from a plastic washing-up bowl, equipped with a wire lid which simply slides on and off. Note the attachment for fixing a water spout.

as a basis for a mating cage or a hospital cage, in which cases they are probably the best designs to use.

MATING CAGE

This is simply a cage into which the two chosen hamsters are placed to mate. It can be any design of cage; many breeders use one of their spare cages for this purpose. I prefer to use an all-glass (or plastic) aquarium. This enables one to observe the hamsters while not disturbing them. Observation is essential in case of fights, which often occur when the female is not receptive to or tires of the male's attentions. A secure lid should always be employed; some aquaria are supplied with suitable lids, while it is possible to buy 'carrying cages' from pet shops, which come complete with a lid and are entirely suitable for this purpose.

It is impossible to list all of the suitable cage designs here, but the foregoing should suffice to help guide you in your choice. Above all, ensure that the cage design(s), size and materials are practical and long-lasting, and that you always have sufficient cages to house *all* of your stock comfortably. It is no fun having to run around making cages while members of a young litter (that should have been separated several days ago) fight each other and their mother. Plan your every move, and you will enjoy your hamstery for many years.

Wood shavings and bedding

Whichever type of cage you choose, the floor should be covered with about 20mm (¾in) of wood shavings. Do not use sawdust, as this fine material can easily be breathed in by the hamster, causing respiratory problems.

The type of bedding used must be given some consideration, too. Although some authorities will argue that, as it is natural, hay is the best material for the hamster's bedding, this is not true. Hay carries dust (and sometimes disease and parasites such as mites) and so should *not* be used. It is far better to use a paper-based bedding. There are several types on the market which are made from material classed as being completely biodegradable, and manufactured from good-quality material. This material is non-toxic, can be digested (hamsters always nibble at their bedding) and is easy and cheap to obtain. Some synthetic hamster beddings can cause problems because, when the animal inevitably swallows it, it builds up in the intestines, causing a blockage. Although this blockage usually only results in mild constipation, in some more severe cases it can lead to a complete prolapse, leading to a long agonizing death for the unfortunate hamster.

Other requirements

Water

When they were first introduced, many people assumed that, as hamsters were desert creatures, they would not require water. However, every living thing needs water. The old argument used to be that the hamsters would get their moisture from greenstuff and other plant materials that they were fed on. While this may be true to a certain degree, I still prefer to give water to all of my stock. I do know of several fanciers who, for many years, have not given water to their hamsters, and yet those hamsters are all in excellent condition and regularly win shows! This is not, however, a practice that I would encourage.

The water should not be supplied in dishes, as these are very easily tipped over and/or soiled by the hamster. Instead, it is best to use sealed water bottles which work by gravity. These are sold in pet shops as small animal water bottles and come in various sizes. Choose the ones intended for rats and hamsters, rather than those sold for mice, as the latter will not contain enough water to last a hamster for more than a day or so. Alternatively, you can buy the spouts separately and, by using the correct rubber bung, adapt empty soft-drink bottles of suitable size. Avoid, if at all possible, the use of glass bottles, as these are too easily broken, with the risk of injury to you and/or the hamsters.

Whichever type of water bottle you choose, pay particular attention to the material from which the spout is made. Some are manufactured from aluminium, and this material is totally useless for this purpose *unless* the end of the spout is covered with a steel jacket. Better still, choose a spout made entirely from stainless steel, as this will withstand all the gnawing that a hamster is likely to give it. A ball-bearing fitted in the end of the spout will help to ensure that the water is delivered efficiently, and also reduce the risk of dripping water, which will eventually flood the cage. Better-quality drinking spouts are equipped with a double ball-bearing, but consequently are more expensive, although I consider it to be money well spent, and an investment.

Periodically, the water bottles must be cleaned thoroughly using a bottle brush and a mild bleach, such as the sterilizing fluid designed for cleaning human babies' bottles. This will help prevent the growth and build-up of algae, small green plants which thrive in the conditions found in these water bottles. These algae can cause tummy upsets in stock and so need to be kept to a minimum. This thorough cleaning should be done at least once every other week.

All cages will require water bottles. These can be fixed to the cage in a variety of ways. The simplest involves the drinking bottle being hung on the outside of the cage, with the spout protruding through the wire netting at a convenient height for the cage's occupants. If the cage is high enough, the bottle may be fixed on the inside of the cage. This latter method, however, can cause a few problems, not least of all the fact that the hamster will undoubtedly attack the bottle, damaging it and perhaps flooding the cage at the same time. This can be avoided by placing the drinking bottle itself in a protective wire cage. This, however, will cause problems of its own as the cage will then be difficult to clean, and the refilling of the water bottle will be anything but simple. Don't make life more difficult for yourself; keep the water bottle on the outside of the cage.

Furniture and toys

Some breeders supply their hamsters with a separate nest box, as mentioned earlier, and also some branches to climb on, There is nothing wrong with this, but it is not essential. Hamsters always like to choose the exact location of their nest, and this is not always where their human owner may wish it to be, even if a nest box is provided! The hamster will also climb on the bars of the cage, even if you supply branches. The branches are, however, good for the hamster to chew on, and may well help limit the amount of time (and hence damage) that it spends chewing the cage itself. The hamster will, nevertheless, also chew on the cage bars (referred to as nagging). Exercise wheels provide a means by which hamsters can run off their surplus energy, but they must be chosen and supplied with care. Never choose ones with open bars, as the hamster's legs can easily fall through, causing bruising, breakage or even amputation. Never supply long-haired hamsters with wheels, as their fur can easily become entangled in the central axle, damaging the hamster. Young litters and pregnant mothers should not be given access to any exercise wheel.

There are also many other 'toys' now offered for sale for hamsters and other small mammals, but these are not necessarily designed for the hamster's well-being, and great care must be exercised in their choice and use. Ensure that there are no sharp edges, that the item is made from non-toxic material, and that there is no danger of your hamsters becoming lodged in the item.

Cardboard egg-boxes, tubes and small cardboard boxes (such as those in which toothpaste tubes are supplied) make ideal 'toys' for hamsters, and are completely harmless to them.

Many authorities advise hamster owners to supply their hamster with an empty jam jar which – according to them – the hamster will use as a toilet. I have tried this with dozens of my hamsters, and not one of them ever used the jar for its intended purpose. Instead, they used it as a food store, a nest, or simply something to climb on. By all means try this for yourself if you wish, but don't be surprised if your hamster does not use it for its toilet. A better idea is simply to clean out the corner furthest from the hamster's nest on a regular basis, as this is the area in which your hamster will undoubtedly urinate.

Cage cleaning

All cages, of whatever design, must be thoroughly cleaned at least once each week. In order to do this effectively, some utensils will be required:

a) A scraper, such as is sold in decorating shops for the removal of paint and/or wallpaper. This is ideal for scraping out the soiled shavings from cages.

b) A good stiff-bristled brush, such as a scrubbing brush, which will ensure that all residue is removed.

Care should be taken in the corner(s) which the hamster uses as a toilet. Unless this corner is kept scrupulously clean, it will become discoloured, and the build-up of material will be a breeding ground for disease.

All soiled bedding and wood shavings should be disposed of carefully, in order to avoid smells and the threat of disease. Burning in a garden incinerator is an ideal method.

Use a mild disinfectant for washing the cage (including the wire sections). Ensure that the cage is rinsed (to remove any remnants of the disinfectant) and dried well before putting the hamster back into it.

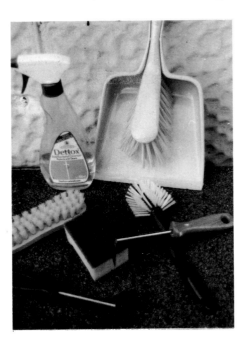

Cleaning utensils such as these will be essential in order to keep the hamstery neat and tidy and prevent the accumulation of shavings etc. The scraper and small brush will be ideal to clean cages.

CHAPTER 4

Feeding

While it is true that no amount of 'fancy diets' will ever produce good stock from poor parents, it is also true that poor or inadequate feeding can and will ruin good stock, regardless of their breeding. It is obvious, then, that we must carefully choose the diet for our hamsters, if we are to consistently produce healthy specimens which will regularly win cards, rosettes and trophies on the show bench. Before discussing the actual food-stuffs, we first need to understand the meaning of a balanced diet and its constituents.

BALANCED DIETS

A balanced diet is one that gives the recipient all that is required to maintain him/her in good health and condition. Some types of food constituents need the presence of others (to act as catalysts and/or reactants) in order for the body to be able to use them. The constituents of a balanced diet can be summed up as:

a) Proteins,
b) Carbohydrates and fats,
c) Vitamins,
d) Minerals,
e) Water.

Proteins

Proteins are necessary for growth and tissue-building and are, therefore, essential to all hamsters, but are even more important for young stock and pregnant mothers. Good sources of protein are cheese, meat, fish, eggs and milk. However, hamsters are notorious hoarders and so these items can only be fed sparingly as, if stored, they would soon turn sour and rot. Better foods for our purpose are barley, beans, maize, nuts, oats, peas and wheat.

Carbohydrates and fats

Both carbohydrates and fats provide energy and warmth. However, if fed in excess, they are stored in the body as fat and this can cause breeding problems and ill health. For this reason, avoid giving too much of these two substances in the hamsters' diet. Carbohydrates are contained in sugar, yeast, potato and milk. Both carbohydrates and fat are contained in barley, maize, oats and wheat.

Vitamins

Vitamins are only required in very small amounts, but are essential for the hamsters' good health. It is usual to refer to vitamins by a letter of the alphabet, and the most common ones are listed below.

Sources of vitamins and effects of deficiencies

Vitamin	Effect of deficiency	Source
A	lack of growth, diarrhoea	carrots, dandelions, fish-liver oils, green vegetables, hay
*B	poor growth, diarrhoea	wheatgerm, yeast, meat, liver
C	scurvy, swollen joints	fresh fruit and vegetables
D	rickets	fish-liver oils, wheatgerm, green vegetables
E	poor reproduction, skin disorders	seed germ oil, wheatgerm, green vegetables

* Vitamin B acts on the nervous system, and a regular dose of this vitamin is thought to be effective in treating stress in small mammals. I always feed all of my stock with one half of a brewer's yeast tablet every week. Stress is one of the main contributory factors in many diseases, especially wet tail; it may well be, therefore, that feeding this extra vitamin B will help prevent many illnesses, including wet tail.

Minerals

Like vitamins, minerals are only required in very small amounts and, as they are contained in milk, vegetables, green foods and grains, it is not necessary to list them here.

Water

Water is essential to all life forms. A constant source of fresh, clean water must be available to every hamster at all times. This is best achieved through a water bottle or similar gravity-fed watering system, since dishes are too easily upset and fouled (see Chapter 3, Housing).

FOODSTUFFS

Mixed grain

It will be obvious by now that almost all of the hamsters' dietary requirements can be met by utilizing a mixture of grains, nuts and pulses. The hard food contained in a mix of this nature will also help to satisfy the hamsters' need to gnaw, thus keeping their teeth in good condition. This type of mix is readily available at good pet shops, but many breeders prefer to mix their own, often jealously guarding their 'secret formulation'. This is partly due to the fact that, as with anything in life, variations exist; while one pet store may sell a good-quality mix, the next one may not. Also, pet-shop mixes tend to vary from week to week. Another very important factor is cost; it is much cheaper to buy the different grains in bulk and mix them oneself than to buy ready-mixed food from a pet shop.

In order to ensure consistent high quality, I recommend that you make your own mix. By buying the constituents in bulk, you will also save money. The list below will give 25kg (55lb) of balanced mixture. You may well wish to add or substitute other items, but remember that we are trying to obtain a *balanced diet*.

Constituents of a balanced diet

Constituent	Weight (kg)	(lb	oz)	Proportion (per cent)
Puppy meal (with cod-liver oil)	6	13	4	24
Sunflower seeds	3	6	10	12
Peanuts	2	4	7	8
Mixed corn (wheat, barley etc.)	7	15	7	28
Flaked peas	1	2	3	4
*Rolled oats	3	6	10	12
*Flaked maize	3	6	10	12

*As these ingredients are 'heating foods', this figure should be halved at any time other than during the winter.

This mixture will provide a good foundation for your stock's diet, but it must be supplemented with the other foods that are listed on p.80.

Mixed bird seeds

The seed sold for birds, such as budgerigars and canaries, is also ideal as a supplement to the mixed grain already mentioned. It can be either mixed in with the main food, or added to the diet in the form of one teaspoonful per week, sprinkled over the hamsters' other food.

Fruit and vegetables

Obviously, the list of foods under this heading could easily fill many pages of this book. However, I list here those items which are easily available to most hamster keepers. Although common names differ in some countries, the interested reader should be able to identify the fruit and vegetables listed below.

Suitable foods

Acorns	Chicory	Parsley
Apples	Chickweed	Parsnip
Asparagus	Chinese cabbage	Pears
Banana	Clover	Peas (all types including
*Beet (only feed raw,	Common vetch	reconstituted dried
NOT cooked or	Corn-on-the-cob	peas)
pickled)	Courgettes/Zucchini	Plantain
Bean sprouts	Cucumber	Potato
Beans (all types, but	Cress	Spinach
not raw red kidney	Dandelions (both the	Strawberries
beans)	leaves and the	Swede
Broccoli	flowers)	Sweetcorn
Brussel sprouts	Grapes	Sweet potato
Cabbage	Groundsel	Trefoil
Calabrese	Kale	Turnip
*Carrots	Lettuce	Watercress
Cauliflower (all parts)	Marrow/Squash	Young grass
Celery	Melon	
Chestnuts (NOT horse	Orange (including	
chestnuts)	tangerines etc.)	

*Although some authorities cite carrots as being fattening, this is not true. However, feeding either beet and/or carrot will cause some discoloration of the coat, and so they should not be fed to white varieties. This discoloration arises in the same way as it does in flamingoes, where the carotene from the animals on which they feed affects the hair follicles, turning the feathers pink. This effect can, however, be used to the advantage of any one breeding golden, cream, cinnamon or similar coloured hamsters, as the extra colour will enhance the animal's appearance.

All of the above items should be fed raw. *All* fruit and vegetables must be washed prior to feeding it to your stock. Wild items must be picked from areas that are free from other animals, to avoid feeding food that has been fouled; even so, they must still be thoroughly washed before offering them to your stock and, if necessary, then dried to prevent mildew or rotting. Failure to observe these commonsense rules will result in sick – and perhaps dead – hamsters.

Fig. 15 Common chickweed. **Fig. 16** Common birdsfoot trefoil.

Fig. 17 Clover.

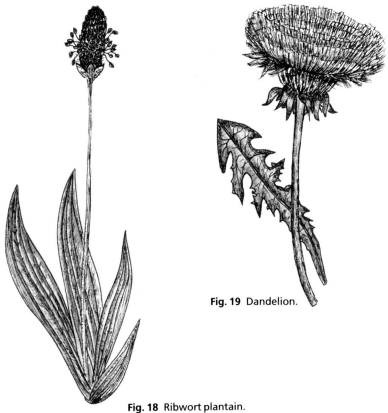

Fig. 19 Dandelion.

Fig. 18 Ribwort plantain.

Unsuitable foods are, again, too numerous to give an exhaustive list. The foregoing list gives only foods which I have fed to my own stock for many years, and which, therefore, you can safely feed to your stock. However, below are some of the more common foods which must *not* be fed to hamsters.

Unsuitable foods

Buttercups
Deadly nightshade
Evergreen leaves (or any part of such trees as laurel, privet etc.)
Hemlock
Henbane
Oak leaves
Toadflax

Eggs

Hard-boiled eggs are relished by hamsters and, as they contain so much goodness (as described elsewhere in this chapter), they are to be recommended for feeding to all stock, especially pregnant/nursing mothers and young stock. Take care not to feed egg too often, and ensure that any not eaten is removed within 24 hours, to prevent the hamster from eating bad or decayed food. There is a school of thought that indicates that feeding raw eggs to hamsters can cause loss of fur and even total blindness, and so it is a wise precaution not to feed raw eggs to your stock.

Milk

Some breeders give milk to their stock, particularly youngsters and pregnant and nursing mothers. The only way to feed milk to your stock, however, is to give it in a dish, which can all too easily be tipped up or soiled. Milk also turns sour very quickly in warm weather, or in a warm hamstery, and so great care must be taken. Only give small amounts at a time, and ensure that all dishes are regularly removed and cleaned thoroughly. Even with these possible disadvantages, the feeding of milk to stock, particularly expectant and nursing mothers, young pups and sick animals is recommended.

Fish-liver oils

These oils are rich in vitamins A and D, and so a few drops on the hamster's grain once every week will prove beneficial. As will have been noticed in the recommended grain mix, it is possible to buy puppy meal that is already impregnated with cod-liver oil, and this is an excellent way of providing this food. Small pieces of fish can also be given, but remember to remove any uneaten pieces before they have time to decay.

Meat

The feeding of meat to hamsters has been a matter of great debate for many years. Some breeders insist that the practice will give the hamster a taste for flesh, and thus encourage cannibalism. I cannot agree with this. For over 30 years, I have fed my hamsters on a diet which includes pieces of raw meat and live mealworms, and I have never seen any evidence to support the 'meat = cannibalism' theory. Rather, the evidence has gone against this theory (including reports that some of the first hamster colonies were fed on a diet consisting almost entirely of meat, with no adverse effect), and so I recommend that you feed your stock with small pieces of beef or mutton. Pork should, however, be avoided.

A particular favourite with hamsters is the mealworm, sold as live food for reptiles, birds, primates and other animals, and now widely available in pet shops. These maggot-like creatures (the larval form of the meal beetle) are an excellent source of both vitamins A and D) and protein. The worms must be stored at a cool temperature (about 8°C or 48°F is the optimum) in order to prevent them from meta-morphosing into beetles (hamsters will not eat the beetles). The mealworms must also be kept dry and in a well-ventilated container. Bran or a piece of dry bread, along with a small amount of lettuce or cabbage, will supply the food for the mealworms.

SPECIAL DIETS

Some hamsters will require a special diet, due to their condition, e.g. pregnant and nursing females. For this reason, I list below some methods of providing these animals with the extra vitamins and other nutrients that they will need. I do not, however, recommend anyone to make a habit of feeding elaborate diets since, as stated earlier, this cannot improve poor stock. Such practice also makes life more difficult, with the result that, all too often, the breeder finds hamstering too much work and so gives up the Fancy. If you keep life simple (while, of course, ensuring that your stock is well cared for), you will enjoy the hobby much more.

Pregnant and nursing females

These animals need a high-protein, vitamin-enriched diet. Mix equal amounts of a top-quality powdered baby-milk with medium oatmeal and wheatgerm meal. Even better, use a complete diet food/drink designed for human adults, in place of, or in addition to, the baby-milk. This mixture should be kept dry (store in an airtight container) until use. To feed, you can either sprinkle about one teaspoonful of the dry mix on to the hamsters' mixed grain, or you can add a little milk, mix well, and feed in a small pot. If using the latter method, do not give too much at any one time, since the hamster will store it, and it is likely to go off, giving the hamster an upset stomach or worse.

New-born pups

When the pups are about 4–5 days old, they will benefit from some of the aforementioned mix being sprinkled in the nest and on the pups themselves. They (and the mother) will lick this off and, in so doing, will take in the extra goodness supplied. The pups will start eating green vegetables from about 7–9 days of age, and so you should place a small amount of finely chopped cabbage, dandelion and/or lettuce leaves in the nest at this age. Again, the mother will also eat these little extras.

Growing stock

Once stock is weaned, it is important to ensure that they continue to get all of their dietary requirements if they are to grow into strong, healthy adults. Such young stock requires more protein than older animals, and so it is worthwhile supplementing their normal food with such items as fresh or dried pulses (beans and peas etc.), small pieces of cheese, fish and eggs, but remember that hamsters love to store all foods. Only give sufficient of these perishables for the hamsters to eat them on the same day, checking for, and removing, any leftovers within 24 hours.

OTHER FOODS

Dog and cat foods

Many dogs and cats are today fed on complete diets which come in two main formats – pellets/biscuits or a muesli-like mixture. These are excellent to *supplement* the hamsters' diet, but must not be used as the basis of a diet – a dog's requirements are different from those of a hamster and, although the diet may well seem to work OK for a while, the stock will gradually deteriorate. Unfortunately this deterioration will be so gradual that it may be several generations before you notice that your stock is not what it used to be! The first signs are usually loss of size and vigour. Play safe and give a proper *balanced* diet to your hamsters, and you will reap the long-term rewards.

Dog biscuits are a good way of giving your stock a healthy nibble which, at the same time, will also keep their teeth in shape, preventing them from becoming overgrown. Feed one of these biscuits (30mm/ 1¼in in diameter) to each hamster once a week.

Titbits

All animals enjoy a tasty morsel now and then, and hamsters are no exception. There is no harm in this, provided that you do not overdo it; 'a little, often' is a good rule, rather than a lot at infrequent intervals.

Raisins, sultanas, Brazil nuts, dog biscuits and suchlike are all relished by hamsters and will also provide extra nutrition. *Never* feed any chocolate, sweets or similiar substance to hamsters, as they will inevitably pouch some of it, with the danger that some will get stuck and damage the delicate inner lining of their cheek pouches. These injuries often prove difficult – if not impossible – to treat, and the hamster is likely to die.

Mash

During colder weather, hamsters appreciate an occasional warm mash, especially if they live in unheated quarters. This mash can be made from household scraps (potatoes, vegetables, meat etc.) or can consist entirely of one of the proprietary brands of complete dog or cat food. Again, it is important to remember that such food will quickly sour and so only small amounts should be fed on any one occasion. Do not use raw egg in such a mash. Even in very cold weather, mashes must not form the main diet for a hamster.

FEEDING TIMES

Hamsters need only be fed once each day and, in order to provide them with useful activity, the dry food should be sprinkled on the floor of the cage. An adult hamster requires about one tablespoonful of dry food each day, plus some of the other items that I have listed earlier. Check regularly to ensure that every hamster has enough food to maintain its store, without which it will not be content.

By feeding your hamsters with a well-thought-out balanced diet at all times, you will help ensure that your stock grows at a good rate and is healthy.

CHAPTER 5

Breeding

If you are serious about your hamsters and the Hamster Fancy, it will not be long before you start to think about breeding your hamsters. However, before you actually embark on this course of action, you should sit down and think seriously about the whole thing. Why do you wish to breed your stock? Which animals should you use? How will you house the young pups? How will you dispose of those that you will not wish to keep? Where will you house those that you do wish to keep?

The answer to the first question should be that you wish to improve your current stock and establish and perpetuate your own line. The answer to the second question must be 'the very best hamsters available to me'. As you will already know, you will also require a *minimum* of two spare cages in which to house the litter (males in one, females in the other) *plus* extra cages for any of the litter that you intend to keep – all hamsters need separate cages from about 8–10 weeks of age. Of course, all of these cages must be available and ready *before* the actual mating takes place, thus eliminating the need for a last-minute struggle to build or buy them, which will inevitably mean that the stock is subjected to the stress of not being housed adequately.

Local pet shops should be sounded out about the possibility of their taking your surplus stock, and only when you are certain that you can easily and efficiently dispose of this surplus should you take your breeding plans any further. It is unlikely that you will be paid very much for these animals, but most shops will give more value if you offer to take goods (e.g. hamster food) instead of cash. At this stage in your hamstering career, it is doubtful that your surplus stock will be suitable to sell to other breeders/exhibitors, since you will wish to keep all of the best progeny for your own hamstery. If you have borrowed a male hamster as a stud, you should make definite arrangements for the purchase of that service *before* the actual mating. This aspect is discussed in full later in this chapter.

METHODS OF BREEDING

Line-breeding and inbreeding

Inbreeding is the mating together of closely related animals, e.g. mother to son, father to daughter, brother to sister. There is a commonly held belief that inbreeding is highly undesirable, resulting in poor stock and small litters. This is not true. *Controlled* inbreeding is the method that has been used for countless generations to produce champion horses, cattle, dogs, hamsters (remember that the original stock, from which the vast majority of today's hamsters have descended, came from one family) and many other species. The only dangers with inbreeding occur when there is little or no control. Controlled inbreeding will fix good characteristics and bring out others which are not readily apparent.

Line-breeding is a less acute form of inbreeding, in which more distantly related animals are mated, e.g. cousins, grandparents to grandchildren etc.

New colour mutations are more likely to appear through inbreeding, as there is more likelihood that both animals in a mating will possess the same recessive mutant gene (for more details see Chapter 6, Genetics).

In practice, most breeders use a combination of the two methods. I use two distinct lines for each variety. Both are distantly related, but inbred within each line for several generations, at which time I will use an outcross (the use of a totally unrelated hamster) to the other line. To my mind, this method gives the best of both worlds.

Fixing features

Certain features – size, type, colour and markings, fur, eyes and ears – will influence the judge at a hamster show, and make the difference between winning and losing (see Chapter 7, Exhibiting, for more details). Some stock are outstanding in one area, e.g. type, while lacking in another, e.g. size. Very few hamsters are anywhere near 'perfect', i.e. possessing all of the necessary good features.

Obviously, then, the breeder will wish to ensure that all good features are fixed, i.e. they will always be retained, while other features are worked on. As an example, supposing you have a dark golden hamster with a perfect hairline chestband, vital if he is going to get good marks in the Colour and Markings category. He must be mated to a female who also possesses such a chestband. Both should also possess as many other desirable characteristics as possible. The first generation from this mating (F1, see p.105) may or may not all possess the perfect chestbands of their parents, but the best of the litter (at least one of each sex) should be retained. These two animals should then be mated back to their parents, i.e. the male to his mother, and the female to her father.

The next generation (F2) should contain several animals possessing the excellent chestband or, at the very least, chestbands which show a marked improvement over those in the F1 generation. Again, select hamsters with the best chestbands (a minimum of one male and one female), and mate these back to their parents. All of the resulting litter (F3 generation) will now show obvious improvements in their chestbands.

A word of warning; the above method will also fix bad characteristics, and so none of the animals selected for breeding must possess the same faults as the other in the mating.

Your ultimate aim must be to produce a line of perfect hamsters which, in turn, will produce more perfect specimens. In order to do this, you next have to combine several good features, so that you can begin winning at shows. It is usual to concentrate on two main features at the same time, waiting until they are successfully fixed before passing on to the next. All through this time, you must also keep a very wary eye open to ensure that you do not also fix one or more bad features in your line. All of the details must, of course, be recorded.

Taking our earlier example, you may find that you now have well-marked individuals but while some have good type, others which do not have good type possess good, dense fur. If you were to mate two of these animals together, the progeny (F1) would probably have type and fur that lies about mid-way betweem that of the good parent and that of the poor parent, i.e. all would be mediocre.

The way to combine these two desirable features (in this case type and fur) is to select the best brother and sister from the F1 generation, mating them together. Even better is to mate several pairs from the F1 generation, or else breed several litters from the same pair. The idea is to produce a large F2 generation which, by the law of averages, will contain several hamsters possessing both good type and good fur. Only the very best progeny must be used for further breeding if the exercise is to be successful and therefore worthwhile.

Your breeding will inevitably expose a large number of hitherto hidden faults, which need to be eliminated, as a by-product of your fixing the two chosen characteristics. If no good stock is produced by the F2 generation, then you must start again. When you have combined these good features, repeat the whole process until all of the hamsters' features are good enough to win shows. Remember that only through strict selection and highly controlled breeding will you arrive at your target – hamsters which consistently produce excellent stock, capable of winning classes at shows and taking home Best in Show awards on a regular basis.

Dangerous genes

Amongst the genes carried by hamsters are some which have potential dangers in some circumstances. For instance, the satin gene (Sa), while perfectly 'safe' when combined with a *normal* (i.e. unsatinized) gene, if combined with another satin gene has the effect of creating thin fur. This phenomenon is known as *super-satinization* and, if such animals are bred together, they will eventually produce hamsters which are completely bald except for a thin covering of very fine hairs.

Likewise, the gene which is responsible for some strains of the black-eyed white hamster (Wh), and all white-bellied hamsters, can cause young to be born without eyes. The gene is known as *anopthalmic* – meaning eyeless, and is recessive, which means that it will not normally show up. However, if both hamsters in a mating carry this gene, then approximately 25 per cent of the litter will be born without eyes. While it could be argued that hamsters generally have poor eyesight and so blindness is not in itself cruel, the traumatic effect on a young child of producing such handicapped pups need not be stated here. Most hamster clubs try to dissuade their members from breeding any hamster with the Wh gene, as most of the colours that have been bred using that gene can also be bred by using others which do not have any deleterious effect (e.g. the black-eyed white can be bred using the dominant spot gene Ds).

The foregoing is explained in more detail in the following chapter on genetics.

SELECTION OF BREEDING STOCK

There is an old stockman's saying about breeding animals that is as true for hamsters as it is for cows, horses, dogs or any other type of animal: 'Put the best to best, and hope for the best!'.

Hopefully, you will have some good hamsters in your possession. Better still, you will own several hamsters that have won awards at hamster shows, including the coveted title of Best in Show. These are the type of animals that you need to breed from. If you have no animals of this calibre, then you should seriously consider buying young stock with winning potential rather than breeding your own animals from mediocre stock, since, to quote another adage, 'you will only get out what you put in'. In other words, poor stock bred with other poor stock will only produce more poor stock.

A halfway house between breeding your own hamsters from your own stock and buying hamsters that another breeder has bred, is to borrow a top-grade male (a stud) to mate with one of your females (the male in a mating is known as the *sire*, while the female is known as the *dam*). This female must, of course, be of a high standard, or you will simply be wasting your time. As mentioned earlier, you will probably have to pay some price for the stud services of the male (although some breeders will give you this service for free, simply because they value the Hamster Fancy and wish to encourage newcomers). The payment for these services can be cash, but is usually 'pick of the litter', which can mean up to 50 per cent of the litter. Unfortunately, if the supplier of the stud wishes to obtain good exhibition stock (just as you do), he will almost certainly choose the best of the litter, leaving you with the rest. For this reason, most breeders (myself included) will supply a stud service free of charge on the understanding that, at a later unspecified date, if they need a similiar service or some new young stock, you will provide these at the same rates – i.e. free.

If you do not know whether the animals that you possess are good, bad or indifferent (because you have never entered them in a hamster show), then you should ask an experienced breeder/exhibitor for his opinion. Failing that, carefully read the standards set out by the Hamster Fancy (see Chapter 7, Exhibiting), and compare your hamsters to these standards. However, it has to be said that reading about a subject is not as good as having firsthand experience of it. Contact your local hamster club and attend a show, and talk to experienced breeders/exhibitors about your stock and what makes a good hamster. Remember that each variety will have a different standard for its colour and markings, but all hamsters have the same standards relating to size, type, condition, eyes and ears. Remember also that individual clubs and judges will interpret the standards slightly differently from each other, and so you should try to visit shows in other areas of the country, rather than merely staying in your own locality.

Suitable age

Hamsters can mate and conceive at the incredibly early age of 28 days, but this is not to be recommended as it is unfair to the female, and the resulting litter will be small and of poor quality. This characteristic does, however, explain why many hamsters bought from pet shops and inexperienced breeders will deliver a litter within a week or so of being purchased.

Some breeders will breed from their stock at 12 weeks of age but, as a rule, I never breed from my stock until they are at least 4 and preferably 6 months old. To my mind, this gives the hamster plenty of time to mature, and the animal's full potential – temperament, type, colour and markings – can all be seen. True, this course of action does limit the number of litters that any one female can produce, but I consider that to be worthwhile, since I am after quality and not quantity. The one exception to this rule is where a 'new' colour or variety has been produced, and it is essential to produce many more examples in order to ensure that the particular mutant strain does not die out.

The female should not be bred from until at least 3 months after the birth of her last litter. Males can also be used too often and so mating should be limited to no more than once or twice a week, with a completely empty week at least once every month. On average, females become barren at about 12 months, while males are usually infertile by 18–20 months. All hamsters used for breeding, and in particular the males, should be fed with extra vitamin E for several weeks before the mating; stud males should consistently have extra vitamin E added to their diet throughout their active life. Their diet should also be high in protein.

Oestrus cycle

A female hamster can only mate at certain times, a feature that is common to many animal species; these times are termed as her period of oestrus, during which she is said to be *on heat* or *in season*. If a female hamster is placed with a male hamster when she is not on heat, a fight is likely to result – often with disastrous results for the male, as females have been known to seriously injure or even kill males at such time, if no human intervention is forthcoming.

The period of oestrus occurs every fourth night (although some hamsters do occasionally slip a day or two), lasting from dusk until dawn during the summer months, but only for a couple of hours during the winter, and is influenced by the ratio of daylight hours to night-time. This phenomenon is known as *photoperiodism* and, in the wild, will limit the hamster to producing litters only during a specific breeding season, i.e. when the days are long and the nights are short – spring and summer. This is Nature's way of ensuring that litters are only born during the spring and summer – times when there will always be a plentiful supply of food to feed the extra hungry mouths. In captivity, this is still true but, by extending the hours of daylight using a controlled artificial light source, we can trick the hamsters into believing that it is continually summer, and so it will then be possible to breed hamsters all year round. The minimum is a 14-hour day, while the ideal is an 18-hour day with a 6-hour night.

Using a time switch, two 60W bulbs can be fixed to come on a few hours before dawn, go off just after dawn, come on again just before dusk and then go off for the night. If you find 8pm a convenient time to attend to your hamsters then, knowing that a female's oestrus begins at dusk and that she will be most receptive to a male approximately 30 minutes after nightfall, the following times will be suitable:

a) 2.00am – light on,
b) 9.00am – light off,
c) 3.00pm – light on,
d) 8.00pm – light off.

Obviously, these times can be altered to suit individual requirements and times of dusk and dawn. They should also be changed in areas where, twice a year, the time is changed by adjusting clocks forward or backwards by one hour.

The addition of a constant low heat will also prove beneficial, especially to the male hamster. During cold weather, his testicles will be drawn up into his body and, at such times, he is not so fertile. Males used for stud purposes should be kept in warm conditions – about 18–20°C (64–68°F). As you will have to supervise the matings, warm conditions in the hamstery will also make life more comfortable for you.

Signs of oestrus

It is impossible to predict accurately on which night certain females will be on heat. The only way to find out for certain is to place a female with a male and, if she is in oestrus, she will *stand* (as discussed in the next section). It is sometimes possible, with some female hamsters, to ascertain whether they are on heat by gently stroking their backs, especially if they can smell a nearby male hamster. This method is not, however, infallible.

THE MATING

Once you have made your selection of the hamsters that you wish to breed from, and have also carried out all of the other preparatory work detailed earlier in this chapter (e.g. arranging spare cages, disposal of stock etc.), you are ready to place the couple together for the actual mating. For this purpose, you will require a mating or 'honeymoon' cage. This can be a standard keeping cage, an old aquarium or any other type of cage. It is important, however, that it is clean and does not smell of any other hamster. *Never* place the male in the female's cage for the mating, since she will then see him as an invader and attack him. The honeymoon cage should also have about 25cm (11in) of wood shavings on the floor and a securely fastening lid. It must not contain any bedding, food or furniture of any kind.

Place the male in the cage first and then, holding the female, allow the male to sniff at the female's sex organs before placing her in the cage. This will have the effect of getting the male interested in the female and, if the female is on heat, of also preparing her. If she is on heat then, within a couple of minutes, she will stand stock-still, hind

This sequence of three photographs shows: **1.** A male hamster in the early stages of mating. Notice the 'frozen' stance of the female. **2.** The actual mating of a pair of hamsters. **3.** The male hamster cleaning himself after having mounted and serviced the female. He will frequently stop for his toilet.

legs apart, raising her back end off the ground and pointing her tail in the air. This often happens as soon as the male touches her. If the male is experienced, he will then mount her. At this stage, the cage should be securely fastened and the happy couple can be left for 20–30 minutes, unless either party starts to show disinterest before then. During this time, you can busy yourself feeding, cleaning and generally servicing the hamster cages in the hamstery, casting an occasional glance at the mating pair.

The coitus itself is very brief, lasting only a few seconds, but the male will continually repeat this action time after time, sometimes for over 30 minutes. Once the male has entered the female, he will make short convulsive movements and then immediately dismount. He will then usually wash himself (and very often the female too), before again mounting the female.

When you come to separate the pair, the female may remain 'frozen', in which cause you should gently blow on her back, allowing her several more minutes alone before removing her and placing her back in her own cage, which should by then have had a new supply of food placed in it. Both the female and the male will spend a lot of time cleaning themselves thoroughly after a mating.

If you remove the male from the mating cage too early, he may walk around his cage, pushing his belly on the floor, obviously in discomfort. If this happens, place him back with the same female (if she will accept him) and, when mating resumes, leave the pair for a further 10–15 minutes, or until one party or the other begins to show disinterest.

Problems

Fights

The chances of the chosen female being receptive to the male on the first occasion are one in four, and so there is every likelihood that the female will not accept the mating and a fight may break out. You must be prepared for this, and the fight must be stopped as soon as possible in order to avoid any injuries to one or both hamsters. You should also bear in mind that, if you aren't careful, you too could be injured while trying to stop the fight.

When you place the two hamsters together in their honeymoon cage, have a judging board, a small piece of hardboard or similar, or a gloved hand, ready to flick the warring parties apart and then keep them separated until one can be removed. *Never* use a bare hand, as you will inevitably get bitten and/or scratched, while the two hamsters continue to fight each other.

If the female is not on heat, she may press her back end on the floor of the cage, depositing a foul-smelling, creamy substance which the male will spend time smelling and licking. She obviously does this to distract the male, and it usually works for a short time. If you notice the female do this, you must resign yourself to the fact that she is not on heat, and immediately remove her and place her back in her own cage. Failure to do this will inevitably lead to the couple fighting.

A prelude to such a fight is often one or other of the hamsters making a chattering noise, or one standing on its back legs or rolling on to its back with its front legs splayed; sometimes the two hamsters square up to each other. If this happens, then you must remove one of the parties immediately. Unfortunately, many hamsters give no warning at all, simply launching themselves into a fight with frightening and totally unexpected speed. When this happens, you must act immediately. Using the board, split the pair up (by pushing the board between them) and then flick one party to the opposite end of the cage, keeping the board between them until one hamster can be removed from the cage with a gloved hand. Remember that, even if a hamster is usually placid and friendly towards you, it will have just been in a fight and so will be inclined to take it out on you.

Another method of stopping a fight is to throw a handful of shavings on the fighters, which usually stops them long enough for you to separate them. Squirting them with water from a plant mister will also have the same effect. If using such a mister, ensure that it does not contain, and never has contained, any insecticidal agent or similiar substance that could prove dangerous to the hamsters.

Unsuccessful mating

'The best laid schemes o' mice an' men [and hamsters] gang aft a-gley'. Unfortunately, things don't always work out as we would wish, and sometimes hamsters will not mate or, if they do, the female will not become pregnant. When this happens, you must sit down and think carefully about the problems, possible causes, and ways around them.

If the two hamsters will not mate, this could be due to any of the following:

a) Female not being on heat,
b) Ambient temperature too cold for the male,
c) Inexperience of one or both parties,
d) Over-use of the male for stud,
e) Distractions for the couple,
f) Disinterest of one or both parties.

The cure for the first of these problems is to try on at least nine consecutive nights, to allow for any slippage in the oestrus cycle. Remember that all hamsters are more inclined to mate approximately 30–60 minutes after nightfall (or the beginning of the dark period). If you are not extending the hours of daylight by artificial means, then

The author officiating as a judge at a hamster show. The hamster on the judging frame is a cinnamon. Note the use of the adjustable reading lamp, which is fitted with a 'day-light' bulb, thus ensuring that every hamster is judged under the same lighting conditions throughout the show. The young lady on the author's left is the book steward, and is also being trained for future service as a judge.

An inside room used as a hamstery. Note that every cage has an identifying label, and that the shelving is strong and designed for the fancier's needs.

A dark golden hamster waiting for her daily food ration. A healthy hamster should have big, bright eyes, erect ears and be inquisitive.

Provided that they are given enough bedding, hamsters will always adjust their nests to suit the prevailing weather conditions. They will also need sufficient food to enable them to maintain a food store in their nest. You must regularly inspect this store to remove any perishable food that may otherwise go bad.

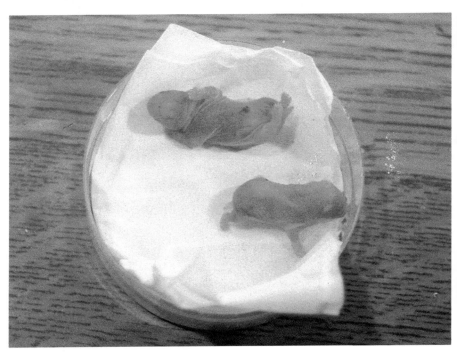

Two hamster pups at 1 hour old. They are naked, blind, deaf and completely dependent upon their mother. Note the umbilicus on the top pup.

Two hamster pups at 1 day old. Already they are showing signs of the dark colouring that their parents had. Their eyes are now clearly visible under the eyelids.

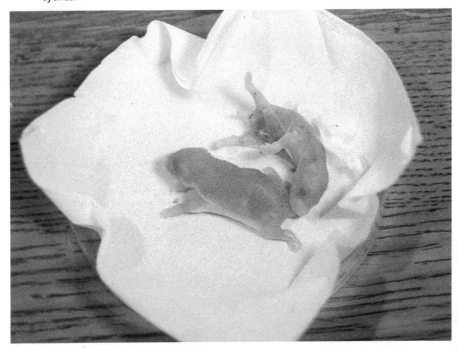

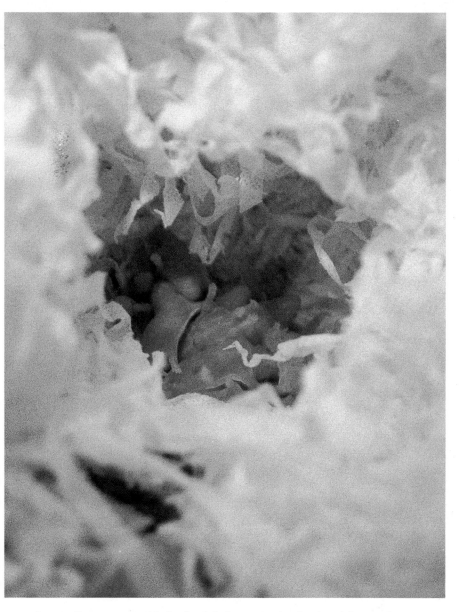

A nest of hamster pups. Mother has left them to gather food, and the opening to the nest has been gently widened to allow this photograph to be taken. Normally, one would not be able to see the pups.

A 3-day-old pup. The colour is now clearly visible, and the pup is quite mobile, often wriggling its way out of the nest, only to be retrieved by the mother.

An 8-day-old pup. Its eyes are still closed, though this will not prevent it from making frequent forays out of the nest. Note the hip spots, which are clearly visible as light coloured dots on the animal's flanks.

A nest of 8-day-old dark golden pups eating solids. Their eyes are still closed, but will open within the next 4 or 5 days.

the female oestrus will occur at about 2.00am during the winter months, and will last only for a very short time. See Chapter 5 for further details.

If you believe that the hamstery is too cold for the male's testes to have descended, try heating the hamstery or, if this is not possible, place both the male and female (in their own cages) in a place where it is possible to maintain a reasonable temperature all day (and all night) through. They should be left in the warmth for about a week before you try mating them again.

If both parties are inexperienced, substitute the male for an experienced hamster. If it is only the male that is inexperienced, try actually placing him on the female when she is standing. Although he may well climb off her several times, he will eventually get the hang of it and mate with her.

If you have used the male regularly over the preceding few weeks, give him a rest for about a fortnight, during which time he should be fed (as should all stud males) on a high-protein diet, with extra vitamin E added. Try him again after this recuperative period.

Never distract the hamsters while they are in their honeymoon cage. Ensure that the cage is free from all smells of other hamsters, and contains no food, bedding or any type of furniture. Place the honeymoon cage in an area where you can check on the hamsters without disturbing them. Try placing the cage in an empty cardboard (or similiar) box, in order that the hamsters cannot be distracted by happenings in the hamstery (e.g. your movements etc.), but so that you can see them from above.

If one or both parties is disinterested in mating, try placing one in the cage of the other for a couple of hours before the mating. Don't expect this to cure the problem overnight, nor to have the desired effect on the first night. As mentioned earlier, it may be necessary to try the pair on up to nine consecutive nights before the female will accept the male's attentions.

If the hamsters have mated successfully but the female is not 'in kindle' (i.e. is not pregnant), then you must start to consider:

a) Did the male actually penetrate the female?
b) Are both animals in good condition?
c) Is the variety concerned noted for low fertility?
d) Is the male physically capable of mating?
e) Was the female a virgin prior to the mating?
f) Is there a dietary deficiency?
g) Is either party too old?

An inexperienced male may not actually penetrate the female during the mating. Overweight hamsters are notoriously infertile, and this extra flesh can also prevent the male from properly servicing the female.

Some varieties are infertile at an early age, particularly the males.

In cold weather, although the male may actually serve the female, he will not be producing enough fertile sperm to fertilize the eggs. Young, immature males may also have the same problem.

Many virgin hamsters require two or more matings before they become pregnant.

The hamsters must be fed a balanced diet. The vitamin E is particularly important for fertility, and males will also require a high-protein diet.

Female hamsters tend to become barren at about 12 months of age, while males become infertile at about 18 months in most varieties, but questions should be asked if either of the hamsters being used is over 12 months of age.

CARE OF MOTHER AND PUPS

Indications of pregnancy

There is no infallible method of testing for pregnancy in hamsters that is available to the average breeder. There are some ways of indicating that the hamster *may* be pregnant or *may not* be pregnant, and the most commonly used indicator is the 'check mating' of the female in question.

Four days after a mating, the couple are again placed together in the honeymoon cage. If the female is receptive, this may well indicate that she is not pregnant. If on the other hand, she is not receptive, this may indicate that she is pregnant. However, I have had females that have accepted matings three times in succession, even though they turned out to be pregnant by the first mating. I have also had females which did not accept a second mating, but still turned out not to be pregnant. I now prefer to wait and see, rather than use these indicators, which very often tell you a false story.

By about the ninth or tenth day of pregnancy, the female will usually show a tell-tale bulge, indicating that she has a litter in her womb. This is the only accurate guide to her condition.

The birth

The hamster has one of the shortest gestation periods (pregnancies) known, and the female usually delivers her litter between 15 and 17 days after mating, usually in the night following the 16th day. Two or three days prior to this, the female's cage must be thoroughly cleaned, and well stocked with extra bedding, shavings and food. The cage will not be cleaned out again until the young pups have their eyes open and

A hamster pup with eyes still closed.

are running around the cage, able to feed themselves (about 12–14 days old). The female should also have been receiving extra rations, plus such items as fruit, vegetables and milk, etc. from about the fourth day after mating, and her diet should contain a higher percentage of protein than normal.

The pups are born blind, deaf, naked and completely dependent upon their mother. Litter size is usually between one and a dozen, with the average being six. Several of my females have delivered – and reared – litters of over 20. It is not necessary to cull (i.e. reduce the size of) litters. The female will know her own limitations and will reduce the number of pups herself if she considers it necessary. It is not true that smaller litters always produce better hamsters than larger litters, provided that all receive adequate nutrition.

Each pup is born singly, covered by a caul (a skin-like membrane), with a few minutes' interval before the next one. The cauls and the other debris of birth are eaten by the mother, helping to replace a lot of the hormones and other important nutrients which have been used for the development of the litter in her womb. This is important and natural; if you see her doing this, under no circumstances must you interfere, or prevent her from eating the afterbirth.

The nest should not be disturbed, even if a newborn pup is seen outside the nest. The mother will soon recover it if all is left alone (or the pup itself may well make its own way back to the warmth of the nest and mother) but, if you disturb the nest, she may well 'defend' her litter in the only way she knows, by killing and eating them.

A female hamster takes food into her nest where she has a litter of 11 pups.

There is no reason whatsoever to look in the nest at this stage, since it will be almost impossible to count the pups and, if anything were wrong, it is almost impossible to hand rear such young hamsters. Some mothers will carry their pups in their cheek pouches; this will not harm the pups and so you should not interfere with her if you see her doing this.

If, after a day or so, you find it imperative to examine the litter, then carefully remove the mother from the cage (but only when she herself has left the nest), and place her in a separate clean cage. Give her lots of food and titbits in that cage, so that she will be too busy pouching all of these goodies to worry about her litter. *Do not* touch the nest with your fingers; instead, use two teaspoons which have just been rubbed well into the shavings covering the floor of the cage, thus acquiring the smell of the cage and its inhabitants. Using these spoons, carefully pull apart the top of the nest just sufficiently to allow you to see the pups. Do not prolong this action; quickly return the nest to its previous condition and, before returning the mother, place still more food in the cage. When you return the mother to her cage, put her directly in front of the food. These actions are designed to distract her from noticing any disturbance of the nest.

A litter of young hamster pups in their nest.

Pup development

By the third day, dark varieties (e.g. golden, black etc.) will begin to show a dark covering of fur, and the ears, which have previously been flattened to their heads, will start to become erect. By the fifth day, the markings on dark varieties will become apparent, while such colours as whites will have a thin covering of light fur.

By the seventh or eighth day, the pups will really resemble tiny hamsters, with a good covering of fur, markings clearly visible and the ears turning grey from the edges on those varieties with dark ears. (Dark-eared albinos are an exception; their ears remain flesh-coloured until the fifth or sixth week.) Hip spots will be clearly seen on all the pups, while the young females will clearly be seen to possess two rows of tiny teats. Although still blind, the pups will be wandering around the cage, and will often be seen holding tiny pieces of food in their front paws while they eat it. Eyes start to open at about day 13. The pups will be weaned at 28 days, and the sexes should be separated and housed in different cages at this time. By the time they are 12 weeks old (and sometimes sooner), they will probably require individual cages, although I like to keep two siblings together for at least two or three more weeks, as I find that this helps the animals to grow.

Feeding

Baby hamsters eat an astonishing amount of food for their size, and you must ensure that there is always plenty for them. This food should also be high in protein (see Chapter 4, Feeding). The mother will also need extra nutrition before, during, and after the pregnancy.

Records

Thorough, accurate record-keeping of all your hamsters, including all details relating to mating and breeding (and any unsuccessful attempts), should be carried out continuously. (See Chapter 2, Selection of Stock, for further details.) Such records are indispensible for fixing a new mutation, or for selecting suitable breeding stock. Using the records carefully, it is possible to select stock that will produce good-quality pups, or even always produce large (or always small) litters.

CHAPTER 6

Genetics

Many people fight shy of genetics, thinking that the subject must be incredibly difficult and that, to understand it, one requires a degree in zoology. Nothing could be further from the truth. Once certain principles have been learned, a few technical terms committed to memory, and a little commonsense applied, the subject will soon be quite easy. Too many people, in the Hamster Fancy and other fancies, will not make this effort, preferring to fumble along, perhaps asking experts for advice from time to time. However, if you do not have a good (i.e. working) knowledge of genetics, your breeding programme will never be more than moderately successful in the long term. At best, you will produce hamsters of average quality, at worst you will produce hamsters that cannot be passed on and yet are useless to yourself.

BASICS

Within the scope of this book, I will attempt to guide the reader only through the basics of the subject. However, once you have grasped those basics, life will be easier and, if you wish, you will be in a position to take your studies further. It is necessary firstly to understand that every animal receives one half of its inherited traits from each parent. Sometimes, for reasons that we shall discuss later, it may seem that some offspring inherit more qualities and characteristics from one parent than from the other, but this is not so.

The inherited components are known as *genes*, which are carried on the *chromosomes*, rather like beads on a string. It is the job of the genes to tell the cells of the body how to behave – to change shape, to grow or to change colour, for instance. In the hamster, there are 44 (22 pairs) of chromosomes. Along this string of beads are points known as *loci* and, normally, each locus is occupied by the same gene.

Sex chromosomes

One pair of chromosomes determines the sex of the individual, and these are logically known as the *sex chromosomes* (all the others are known as *autosomes*). The male chromosome is referred to as Y, while the female chromosome is known as X. A female hamster will have two X chromosomes (XX), and the male will have one X and one Y chromosome (XY). Obviously then, it is the male's chromosomes which influence the sex of any progeny, and the resultant hamster has an equal chance of being male or female.

At fertilization, the germ cells (the female *egg* and the male *sperm*) contain 22 single chromosomes each (due to a process called *meiosis*), so that, on fertilization, the egg (now known as a *zygote*) contains 22 *pairs* again, as will every cell (except the germ cells) of every individual hamster.

The fertilized egg grows and develops into a young hamster. This growth is accomplished by progressive division of the cell, the number of cells doubling at every stage, i.e. 2, 4, 8, 16, 32, etc., until the resultant tissue takes on the appearance of an identifiable foetus. When the cells divide, the chromosomes are *shuffled*, so that the genes which accompany them can form new, as well as established, combinations. It is not known exactly how many genes are carried on a chromosome, but some authorities believe that it could be tens of thousands. Such large numbers are necessary to control all the physiological functions of the body, as each can only act in a very simple manner, and so vast quantities of them are required to control bodily functions.

Mutations

Obviously, the constant creation of new cells means that the chromosomes (and hence the genes) are being constantly duplicated. These duplications usually go according to plan, and the copy made is an exact copy. However, very rarely (about once in a million copies), a slight copying error may occur. This means that a duplicated gene is slightly different from its predecessor. Remember that genes control the functions and appearance of an individual, and so a changed gene could result in a noticeable difference in the animal concerned.

Such an abrupt change, where it results in a change in appearance of the individual, is referred to as a *sport, mutation,* or *mutant*. As far as we, as hamster breeders, are concerned, the mutations that concern us are those which either result in a change in appearance, or have a detrimental effect on the hamsters. When a mutation occurs, thus creating a *mutant allele*, this mutant allele will occupy the same locus as its normal cousin did. During cell division (i.e. growth), some genes may *cross over* from one chromosome to the other chromosome. Genes which are close together on the chromosome will be less likely to cross over than those that are far apart. Two genes on the same chromosome show *linkage*, and the degree of linkage is an indication of the distance between the genes.

MENDELIAN GENETICS

Gregor Mendel was an Austrian monk who, in 1856, carried out a vast number of experiments on hereditary factors. As his subjects, Mendel chose the garden pea (*Pisum sativum*). This plant has a number of easily identifiable characteristics – wrinkled and smooth seeds, long and short stems, red and white flowers, etc. – and he carefully cross-pollinated these and meticulously recorded the results over many years. From these results, Mendel drew several conclusions, and these form the foundations for today's understanding of heredity. He described his work in an obscure natural history journal, in 1866. It wasn't until 1900, however, that the scientific world became aware of Mendel's findings, but today Mendelian genetics form the foundation of all of the work that has been – and still is being – carried out on heredity. We need not dwell on Mendel's experiments with plants too much, as we are discussing genetics relating to the hamster.

All chromosomes, and therefore all genes, are present twice in the individual but only once in the germ cells. At its simplest, genetics concerns the passing on from one generation to the next of several characteristics. In order to grasp the principles involved, we must take the subject one step at a time. We will, therefore, look at the way in which a single characteristic is passed on. This is known as *monohybrid inheritance*.

Monohybrid inheritance

Let us take an example of a pair of *pure* (i.e. true bred) golden hamsters mating together. As all of the inherited material passed on to the next generation must be the same (as regards colour and markings, i.e. golden), then all of the young must also inherit these characteristics. When these hamsters breed with each other, they can again only inherit the same colour and markings.

Suppose, however, that we mated a pure golden hamster with a black-eyed cream. It is obvious that, given that the progeny from any mating will always inherit 50 per cent of its traits from each parent, the litter will all be carrying genes for both golden and black-eyed cream. (The first litter in a series of litters bred for genetic purposes is always referred to as F1, the second as F2, the third as F3, etc., the F standing for filial.) However, some genes dominate others; these are known as *dominant* genes, while those which are dominated, are known as *recessive*. Recessive genes will only show themselves when the animal has two helpings of that recessive gene, i.e. is pure bred. The golden gene, as it is the original (*natural* or *normal*) colour is always dominant to all other colours. Therefore, when the two come together, although the genetic make-up (the *genotype*) of the hamsters is both golden and black-eyed cream, the physical appearance (the *phenotype*) is that of a golden, as the golden gene effectively masks the action of the black-eyed gene.

As in most jobs, practitioners use their own form of shorthand, and the geneticist is certainly no exception. All mutant genes are given a letter; dominant genes are signified by using an upper case (capital) letter, while recessive genes are given a lower case letter. If an animal carrying a mutant gene is mated to an animal *not* carrying that gene, then the shorthand used to designate the hamster not carrying the mutant gene would be the reverse of that for the hamster that *is* carrying that gene, i.e. the shorthand for the gene that produces the black-eyed cream is ee; if such an animal were to be mated with a pure-bred golden, that is obviously *not* carrying that recessive gene, the genotype of the golden would be given as EE. The opposite is also true; if an umbrous hamster (this gene is dominant and so the genotype would be given as UU) was mated to a pure-bred golden hamster, the latter would be given uu as its genotype.

In our example below, the pure goldens would be designated as EE (showing that both sets of genes are the same and that black-eyed cream is recessive to golden), while that of the black-eyed cream is assigned the code ee. Geneticists also use their own method to simplify the way that calculations are carried out. The principle is exactly the same as that used by mathematicians when working out

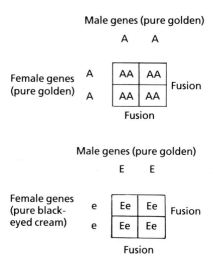

problems involving numbers. The method is known as the Punnett square, and involves the letters representing each set of genes being written along one side and at the top of the square. These are then 'multiplied' together to give the answers in each square.

Where a dominant gene (i.e. one denoted by an upper case letter) is present, it will be this that dictates the phenotype of the hamster. Therefore, in both of the previous examples, all progeny would be phenotypically golden. The resultant young of the mating of two pure goldens have identical genes (i.e. A and A) and are said to be *homozygous* for golden; but the progeny of the mating between the golden and the cream have a gene from the golden (E) and one from the black-eyed cream (e), and are said to be *heterozygous* (split) for cream.

If these splits are self mated (i.e. mated brother to sister), we will see that the recessive genes will now have a chance to show themselves.

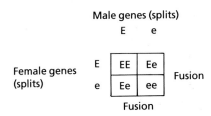

Obviously, those hamsters carrying the ee genotypes will have the phenotype of the black-eyed cream, while those carrying EE and Ee will have a golden phenotype. In all such matings (i.e. between two splits both with the same genotype) approximately 25 per cent of the litter will show the recessive gene in their appearance. This is often expressed as 25:50:25, or 1:2:1, to show the proportions of different genotypes that one would *theoretically* expect to get in the litter. However, it should be noted that any percentages given in genetics are only approximate and, to achieve these types of figures, huge numbers must be bred. This will never be more apparent than in a litter from a mating that produces only a single pup. Whichever phenotype that pup displayed, the actual percentages would be 100 per cent of one and 0 per cent of the others!

Another way of illustrating inheritance involving two hamsters of different genotypes is shown on the next page.

The principles outlined above are very important for breeding good stock and *crossing* to improve a specific line. For example, if you have a line of golden hamsters where all of the animals are of good type and size, but you also have a line of dark-eared albinos that do not possess

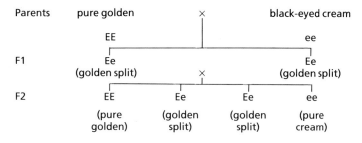

these qualities, you can mate one variety to the other, knowing that, within two generations, you would again be producing pure-bred animals (in the white line).

Dihybrid inheritance

The story is complicated when *both* parents are splits – but not for the same colours. The calculations to solve this problem are carried out in exactly the same way as previous calculations, i.e. with the use of a Punnett square. No matter how experienced you may get, you will never be wasting your time by drawing a Punnett square and working out all of the possibilities on paper, rather than relying totally on mental arithmetic.

Some colours and varieties cannot be produced by 'mixing' others; it is necessary to have one or more animals which are actually carrying the specific mutant gene. Other varieties, however, are obtained from a mix and consequent combination of genes.

If we were to mate a pure-bred fawn (ruru) with a pure-bred black-eyed cream (ee), the fawn would be given the symbol EEruru, while the cream would be given the symbol eeRuRu. All of the progeny of this mating (the F1 generation) would be goldens split for both fawn and cream. If this F1 generation were self mated, golden, cream, fawn, and ruby-eyed creams would be expected to be present in the litter. The calculations are as follows:

F1 Male

		ERu	Eru	eRu	eru
	ERu	EERuRu	EERuru	EeRuRu	EeRuru
F1 Female	Eru	EERuru	EEruru	EeRuru	Eeruru
	eRu	EeRuRu	EeRuru	eeRuRu	eeRuru
	eru	EeRuru	Eeruru	eeRuru	eeruru

The hamsters of genotype EERuRu, EERuru, EeRuRu, and EeRuru will all be phenotypically golden (although only one will be homozygous for golden, i.e. pure bred – EERuRu; all the rest will be heterozygous, i.e. splits – EERuru split for fawn, and the rest carrying cream); those with the genotype EEruru and Eeruru will be fawn; those of genotype eeRuRu and eeRuru will have a cream phenotype, but only the hamster with the genotype eeRuRu will be homozygous, the others being split for fawn.

This mating has produced another colour in addition to those colours (golden, cream and fawn) present at the mating – the ruby-eyed cream (eeruru), although, as this colour only has a one in sixteen chance of appearing, in reality it may not be present. However, if it were, we could improve the chances of the same colour appearing in future generations by carrying out a backcross involving this ruby-eyed cream and a member of the F1 generation (obviously of the opposite sex!).

		F1 Member (EeRuru)			
		ERu	Eru	eRu	eru
F2 Ruby-eyed cream (eeruru)	eru	EeRuru (golden)	Eeruru (fawn)	eeRuru (black-eyed cream)	eeruru (ruby-eyed cream)

This mating increases the chance of a ruby-eyed cream appearing in the litter (to one in four).

Sex-linked inheritance

It will be remembered that it is the male hamster who has both an X and a Y chromosome (XY), while the female has two X chromosomes (XX). If a mutation occurs on either of these two sex chromosomes, it is referred to as *sex*-linked.

In the Syrian hamster, there is only one such gene at present – To – which is responsible for both the tortoiseshell and the yellow varieties, as it extends the yellow pigment in the fur. In a homozygous hamster (ToTo), this will result in a yellow coat, while in a heterozygous hamster (Toto), it will give rise to a tortoiseshell variety. This occurs because of the presence of one normal X chromosome which will limit the effect of that chromosome carrying the To gene, and the yellow colouring will therefore be restricted. For this reason, normally only female tortoiseshell hamsters will ever appear, but both male and female yellows will appear. Very occasionally, a male tortoiseshell will appear, but these are invariably infertile.

Lethal and semi-lethal genes

In some mutations, if the foetus has a double helping of that particular gene, i.e. it is homozygous, the animal dies. These are known as lethal genes. The only such genes currently in circulation in the Hamster Fancy which you are likely to come into contact with are the light grey and the dominant spot. There are others but, as they are either not in general circulation or are limited to laboratories, I will not confuse the issue by listing them here. When these are seen, it can safely be assumed that the animals are heterozygous and, when either of these two varieties are bred together, there will be a one in four chance of any of the resultant foetuses having a homozygous combination of these genes; they will, therefore, die while in the womb, being re-absorbed. Their siblings who survive will not, please note, suffer any adverse effects from the lethal gene.

GENETICS AND HAMSTERS

Having briefly discussed the principles involved, I will now devote space to the specifics of the hamster's genetics.

Coat colours

Scientifically, the normal (i.e. golden) hamster is described as a white-bellied agouti, although the coat colour differs from that of the rabbit and mouse in having more of an auburn tinge (giving it the characteristic colour from which it gained its common name – the golden hamster), and the hamster also has two 'flashes' of dark pigmentation that extend from each shoulder to behind each ear.

   Several genes can affect the coat colour and, while it is not possible to discuss all of them here, I will detail the most common and/or important, in alphabetical order of the genes concerned. Please note that an upper case letter (e.g. U), signifies a dominant gene, while a lower case letter (e.g. r) denotes a recessive gene.

Brown eumelanism (rust)

The rust gene b, produces the rust (or Guinea gold), and can be combined with the dg gene to produce the dove (dgdgbb), and with the e and U genes to give the chocolate (UUeebb).

White band

The Ba (white band) gene produces the white-banded hamster (BaBa or Baba). Whenever it appears in the genotype, this gene will always show itself in the form of a band; although some bands are very thick, almost eliminating the other colours and markings present, others are almost non-existent, giving just a splash of white on the animal. When combined with the To gene, it can produce the tortoiseshell-and-white-hamster (BaBaToto or BabaToto) that is often seen benched at hamster shows.

Acromelanic melanism

The gene cd (acromelanic albinism) is responsible for the dark-eared albino (cdcd), and can be combined with the cinnamon gene (p) to give the albino (cdcdpp). Neither of these animals is a true albino (See Note 2 on page 114).

Recessive grey

The dg gene (recessive grey) produces the dark grey hamster (dgdg), and can be combined with other genes as follows; with the rust gene (b) to produce dove (dgdgbb), the cinnamon gene (p) to produce the lilac (ppdgdg), and the To gene to produce the smoke pearl (ToTodgdg).

Dominant spot

The Ds gene (dominant spot) is lethal when homozygous (DsDs), and so all dominant spot animals seen are obviously heterozygous (Dsds). It produces white spotting on the hamster's coat, in much the same way as the s gene (piebald). However this gene does not produce so much white as the s gene, although it is a better breeder. Combining the Ds gene with the Wh gene will, however, increase the amount of white; this cross is *not* advised, as there is a possibility of producing eyeless whites (see Anopthalmic white). When the Ds gene is combined with the s gene, the variety produced is known as dalmatian (Dsdsss), and is similiar in appearance to the dalmatian variety in the cavy; it is almost completely white, with small patches and spots of colour. Due to the influence of the s gene, this variety is somewhat undersized.

Restriction of eumelanism

The e gene (restriction of eumelanism) produces the black-eyed cream (ee), and can be combined to give other colours such as the red-eyed cream (eepp), the ruby-eyed cream (eeruru), the smoke pearl (ToTodgdg), the black-eyed white (eeWhwh, eeDsdsBaBa, or eeDsds – see Note 1), the roan (UUWhwhee and UUDsdsee – see Note 1 on page 114), the sable (UUee), the caramel (UUeebb), the ivory (Lglgee), and the chocolate (UUeebb).

Light grey

The Lg gene (lethal grey), is responsible for the light grey (Lglg), and can be combined with either the cinnamon (p) gene to produce a red-eyed blonde (ppLglg), or combined with the rust (b) gene to produce a black-eyed blonde (Lglgbb). When combined with the e gene, the resultant variety is the ivory (Lglgee), while the addition of the cinnamon gene, p, will produce a red-eyed ivory (Lglgeepp).

Cinnamon

The p (cinnamon) gene creates the cinnamon hamster (pp) and, by combining with other genes, also creates such colours as the red-eyed cream (eepp), the albino (cdcdpp), the cinnamon fawn (ppruru), the honey (ppToTo), the blonde (ppLglg), the red-eyed ivory (ppeeLglg), the lilac (dgdgpp), the champagne (UUpp), and the caramel (UUeepp).

Ruby-eyed

The ru gene was one of the first mutant alleles to be discovered in the hamster (in 1948), and produces the ruby-eyed fawn (ruru). However, as this variety is rather difficult to breed – the males are frequently infertile, even those that are fertile only remaining so until they are 12–13 weeks old, while the females either lose the young at birth or are very poor mothers, resulting in the litter (or most of it) dying through neglect – they are very rare in today's Fancy. The ru gene can be combined with other genes to produce the ruby-eyed cream (eeruru), and the cinnamon fawn (ppruru).

Irregular spotting

The s gene (irregular spotting) can be combined with most other genes controlling colour type to give a spotted pattern; these animals are known as piebalds. However, piebalds have several disadvantages and drawbacks, not the least of which is their lack of size. Indeed, due to this, many males experience difficulties in mating. Litters are always small, because the young die either before birth or soon afterwards because they are small and weak. Piebalds tend to be more nervous and bad-tempered than other varieties and the females usually make very poor mothers. The spotting from this gene is extremely haphazard and is usually accompanied by brindling. Most breeders wishing to breed spotted hamsters now use the dominant spot gene (Ds). It is impossible to determine accurately which gene is present in any specific hamster without breeding from it, apart from the size factor, i.e. a large spotted animal is almost certainly carrying the Ds gene and not the s gene.

Sex-linked yellow

The gene To (sex-linked yellow) produces the yellow (ToTo) and the tortoiseshell (Toto). It can be combined with the Ba gene to produce tortoiseshell-and-white-hamsters (BaBaToto or BabaToto).

Umbrous

The U gene (umbrous) produces the sooty hamster, as it darkens the saddle on the animal's back as well as the crescents and the stomach, giving rise to a rather dirty-looking golden. However, when combined with the e gene, it produces the umbrous (sable) hamster (eeUU). When combined with both the e and the r gene, the U gene produces the chocolate; with the p gene, it produces a caramel; with the e and Wh genes, it produces the roan (see Note 1).

Anopthalmic white

The Wh gene (anopthalmic white) is a semi-lethal gene, and produces a golden with an almost pure white belly, instead of the usual creamy grey, a difference that is easier to see in the adult than in young stock. The gene also gives a fine sprinkling of white hairs throughout the coat. All white-bellied hamsters are heterozygotes (Whwh), while the homozygote (WhWh) is an eyeless white, i.e. the coat is pure white all over and the eyes are either totally non-existent or rudimentary. Obviously, if the breeder knows what he is doing, he will never mate together two animals carrying this gene, and so eyeless white will never appear in any of his litters. Problems will, however, occur when some stock that is carrying the Wg gene is sold and eventually gets into the hands of a breeder who either doesn't know of the inherent dangers of this gene, or it totally unaware of its existence in his stock. Because of this danger, most hamster clubs try to discourage the use of the Wh gene. The Wh gene can be used in combination with other genes to produce several different varieties such as the black-eyed white (eeWhwh), and the roan (eeUUWhwh), which is a white animal with black eyes and black ticking throughout its coat. Both varieties can also be produced by the use of the Ds gene, accompanied by careful and thoughtful selective breeding, and obviously there is then no danger of any eyeless whites being produced. The latter course is recommended to any reader who wishes to produce roans or black-eyed whites.

Coat types

There are three mutant alleles in circulation in today's Hamster Fancy – the long-haired gene (l), the rex gene (rx), and the satin gene (Sa), all of which can affect the fur of hamsters. Any or all of these can be combined with any of the genes controlling coat colour, e.g. it is possible to produce a satin long-haired rex-banded rust hamster (SasallrxrxBabarr).

Long-hair/Angora

The gene l (long-hair or Angora) produces a long fur, which forms a 'skirt' in good examples; this skirt is, however, only present in males, due to sexual dimorphism, and is due entirely to the lack of the male sex hormone testosterone. This gene also has the affect of diluting the colour and markings of the hamster.

Rex

The gene rx (rex) is a typical rexoid mutant, and the hamster carrying this gene will have curved whiskers and a soft coat with gentle waving. Often the rex hamster will have a thin coat (sometimes even bald patches) and so great care must be taken in selecting stock for breeding, choosing only those hamsters with a full, dense fur. The rex also tends to be undersized, and this point must also be borne in mind when selecting breeding stock.

Satin

The gene Sa (satin) produces a hamster with a bright sheen to its coat, exactly like the sheen seen on satin material. The gene also has the effect of deepening the colour and markings of the animal. Unfortunately, when two satins are bred together, they will produce some 'ultra satins' or 'super satins', which are animals with a thin and straggly coat, and this practice therefore, is not recommended. It is best to breed a satin animal with a normal-coated animal, in which case the litter should consist of 50 per cent normal and 50 per cent satin-coated hamsters.

Notes

1. The Wh gene should be treated with great care, otherwise eyeless whites may be produced. Read the section on the Wh gene very carefully.
2. At present, there is no true albino in the hamster. The dark-eared albino is comparable to the Himalayan varieties in other species, but has no pigment on the points, unlike the Himalayan. It was given its name (in 1952) due to the fact that the animal exhibits partial albinism. The name is entirely self explanatory, and no one should confuse it with the so-called albino. The latter is often referred to as a 'flesh-eared albino', or the 'pink-eared albino' and, like the dark-eared albino, is not a true albino either! It is known as a synthetic albino, and is created using the gene responsible for the appearance of the dark-eared albino (cd) which, when combined with any other diluting gene, reduces the pigment in the ears.

Genes of the Syrian hamster

Symbol	Name
a	Melanistic black
b	Rust or Guinea gold
Ba	White band
cd	Acromelanic albino (dark-eared albino)
dg	Dark or recessive grey
Ds	Dominant spot
dy	Dystrophy
e	Non extension of eumelanism (cream)
f	Frost
hr	Hairless
hy	Hydrocephalus
J	Jute
l	Long-hair or Angora
Lg	Light grey
Mo	Mottled white
N	Naked
*p	Cinnamon (pink-eyed dilution)
pa	Hind-leg paralysis
pi	Pinto
ru	Ruby-eyed
rx	Rex
s	Irregular spotting (piebald)
Sa	Satin
Sg	Silver grey
sz	Spontaneous seizures
T	Tawny
To	Sex-linked yellow or tortoiseshell
U	Umbrous
Wh	Anopthalmic white

*This is thought to be the same gene responsible for the argent in the mouse and gerbil.

N.B. Not all the genes listed are available to fanciers.

Genotypes of some varieties

Genotype	Name(s) of variety
ppcdcd	Albino
eeUU	Black
Lglgbb	Black-eyed blonde
ee	Black-eyed cream
eeLglg	Black-eyed ivory
eeWhwh	Black-eyed white
eeDsdsBaBa	Black-eyed white
ppeeUU	Caramel
eebbUU	Chocolate
pp	Cinnamon (pink-eyed dilution)

cont. overleaf

Genotypes of some varieties

Genotype	Name(s) of variety
Dsdsss	Dalmatian
cdcd	Dark-eared albino
dgdg	Dark grey
dgdgbb	Dove
ppToTo	Honey
Lglg	Light grey
ppdgdg	Lilac
ppLglg	Red-eyed blonde
ppee	Red-eyed cream
eeUUWhwh	Roan
eeruru	Ruby-eyed cream
ruru	Ruby-eyed fawn
bb	Rust or Guinea gold
ToTodgdg	Smoke pearl
UU	Sooty
BabaToto	Tortoiseshell-and-white
Whwh	White-bellied golden
ToTo	Yellow

Date of discovery of mutant genes in the Syrian hamster

Year	Symbol	Name
1947	s	Piebald
1948	ru	Ruby-eyed
1951	e	Black-eyed cream
1952	cd	Dark-eared albino
*1954	Mo	Mottled white
*1954	T	Tawny
1957	Ba	White band
1958	Wh	Anopthalmic white
1958	p	Cinnamon (pink-eyed dilution)
1961	b	Brown (rust)
1962	To	Sex-linked yellow
1963	f	Frost
1964	Dg	Dark grey
1964	Ds	Dominant spot
1965	Lg	Light grey
1969	Sa	Satin
1970	Rx	Rex
1972	l	Long-hair
1973	J	Jute
1975	U	Umbrous
*1977	pi	Pinto

*Year first documented.

CHAPTER 7

Exhibiting

For most readers, exhibition of your hamsters will be the *raison d'être* of your hamstering endeavours. You will be trying to produce a line (or lines) of hamsters that conform as closely as possible to the national standards laid down by the various hamster clubs, hoping that your stock will be regular prize winners at hamster shows throughout the country.

It is therefore necessary to study the standards closely before any breeding is embarked on and, preferably, before any stock is purchased. Standards change from time to time, although the wise hamster clubs do not alter the standards too often, as it is imperative for the Fancy that stable exhibition standards are kept. Without them, it would be impossible for anyone to breed hamsters that conform to the ever-changing standards.

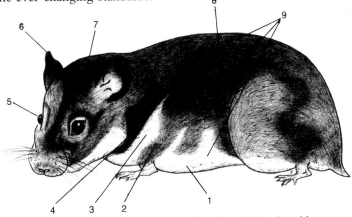

Fig. 20 What the judge is looking for: **1.** Belly fur. **2.** Chestband (not present on all varieties). **3.** Crescent (not present on all varieties). **4.** Cheek flash (not present on all varieties). **5.** Big, bright and prominent eyes. **6.** Large erect ears. **7.** Big broad head. **8.** Top coat. **9.** Fur – must be thick and dense all over the animal. Other points that the judge is looking for are colour and markings, good condition, size (must be large but not fat) and 'type' (the overall shape of the hamster).

STANDARDS

In general, 100 points are allocated for the perfect hamster, and these are apportioned to various categories, i.e. Colour and Markings, Type, Fur, Size, Condition and Eyes and Ears.

Colour and Markings

As the standards are different for each individual variety, these will be detailed later in this chapter. Where possible, I have included a Pantone reference guide, but it must be noted that these are merely a guide.

In the case of a patterned variety, 50 per cent of the marks allocated for this category shall be allotted for colour and 50 per cent for markings. In other varieties the whole allocation of points for this category is taken into consideration.

The following sequence of eye colours (in increasing order of darkness) pertains:

a) Bright clear pink,
b) Red,
c) Claret red,
d) Claret,
e) Garnet red,
f) Ruby,
g) Black.

Type

The type of a hamster is its overall shape (of body and head). The ideal hamster should have a broad and evenly proportioned body, with a large head. The head should ideally be as wide (between the ears) as it is long, and have a blunt muzzle. The head should be well set into the body, giving a smooth curve to the overall shape of the hamster.

Fur

There are three distinctly different types of fur recognized by the Hamster Fancy: normal (short), long and rex, all of which can be bred in either normal or satin coats, and can also be combined with each other, e.g. it is possible to breed a hamster with a satinized, long-haired rexoid coat.

Short-haired hamsters must have fur that is very dense, soft and short. Long-haired hamsters must have hair that is as long as possible, although the female will always have shorter hair than the male (long hair in a female would lead to problems with mating, giving birth and suckling the pups, and so Nature has made allowances). In a good long-haired male, the hair should be about 20–25mm (¾–1in) long, forming a 'skirt' which runs from the neck to the tail on each side of the body. It must be soft and silky, with no matting and no signs of any area that has been cut or trimmed. Rex-coated hamsters must have soft hair that is full of waves, rather like someone who has had a perm. The whiskers of a rex are also curly.

Satinized coats must be fine and glossy, giving the satin sheen after which the variety is named. If a satin is mated to another satin, the fur will be ragged and thin. Satinization tends to increase the depth of colouring on the hamster's coat.

Both long hair and rex coat will have the effect of diluting the colour of the hamster, and so the judge must make allowances for this, as well as for the shorter hair of the female long-haired hamster.

Special attention will be paid to the belly fur, which should be extremely dense.

Size

In general, the hamster should be as large as possible, while not being overweight. The judge cannot penalize any hamster for being too large, but must make allowances for sexual dimorphism, i.e. the female hamster will always have the capacity to grow larger than the male.

Condition

The hamster must be fit and healthy. A hamster in good condition will be curious and active, with bright eyes and a shiny coat. It must not be fat, i.e. all flesh must be firm, with none touching the floor when the hamster is placed on a hard, flat surface. The hamster must be tame, i.e. easy to handle. The hamster will be penalized for any cut, injury or other such damage. The fur of a healthy hamster will have an overall sheen, and the hamster must be clean.

Eyes and Ears

The hamster's eyes must be large and prominent, widely set on the head. The ears must be large, unfolded and carried erect when the hamster is awake. They must be set well apart on the head. Although the judge may penalize the hamster for having pieces missing from the ears, these marks must be deducted from Condition, and not this category. Likewise, the colouring of the eyes and ears is not covered in this section, as it only concerns the size and shape of the eyes and ears. Any penalties for poor colour must be taken into consideration under the Colour and Markings category.

Penalties

All varieties are liable to be penalized for the following:

a) Totally missing limb(s), eye(s) ear(s), foot (or feet), or tail – mandatory disqualification,
b) Disease or ectoparasites – mandatory disqualification,
c) Any physical deformity believed by the judge to be hereditary – mandatory disqualification,
d) Intractibility – mandatory disqualification,
e) Scars, sores or wounds (including missing toes, parts of ears and eye infections) – a maximum of 10 marks may be subtracted under the Condition category,
f) Obesity (excess fat) – a maximum of 5 points may be subtracted under the Condition category,
g) Dirty or stained fur – a maximum of 10 points may be subtracted under the Condition category,
h) Dirty, damaged or badly maintained show pen – a maximum of 10 points may be subtracted from the total points awarded.

STANDARD VARIETIES OF SYRIAN HAMSTERS

The following is a list of the more common varieties that the average breeder/exhibitor will come across. It should be noted, however, that not all of these standards are recognized by all of the hamster clubs throughout the world; some clubs have a more enlightened attitude to possible difficulties involved with some genes (e.g. semi-lethal genes etc.), while some countries have access to colours and varieties which others do not. In particular, some clubs do not wish to encourage the breeding of such animals as the white belly, as it carries the Wh (white bellied or 'eyeless') gene which, if incorrectly used, can result in eyeless babies being produced. As this gene is sometimes also used to produce other varieties in combination with other genes (e.g. the roan), the same clubs will probably not recognize these varieties either. If you are in doubt, consult your own club secretary, who will be happy to give you guidance.

Terms which the reader may come across at a show include 'Agouti' and 'Self'. The agouti is the 'wild type', i.e. the golden (dark, light or normal), while the self is an animal of only one colour, such as the whites, creams or the melanistic black.

In brackets after each standard are the genetic symbols of that variety. The goldens, being the wild-type hamster, do not have symbols as such. However, in order to facilitate genetic calculations, it is common practice to give the goldens the symbols '++'. Any genotype containing one or more of these symbols will have the phenotype (appearance) of a golden. The previous chapter explains this in more detail.

Many of the colours given in the standards are, to say the least, somewhat vague. I have attempted to give my personal interpretation of the colour, and guide the reader. As mentioned, I have also given the Pantone references as a guide only. However, the only true way to discover the exact colours called for in any particular standard is to visit hamster shows, where you will be able to see the hamsters themselves, speak to judges about the colourings that they are looking for (but not while they are judging!), and discuss the practical problems of each variety with those members who have experience of breeding and showing them.

It should be noted that, as stated earlier, some clubs do change the standards from time to time, and so a full list of all the current standards in force at any one time is impossible to print here. The following are, however, representative of the standards recognized by most hamster clubs at the time of going to press, although they are not all necessarily recognized by all clubs, nor is my wording the same as will appear in a club's handbook. Contact your club secretary for full, up-to-date details.

Where 'base colour' is indicated, this applies to the whole animal, excluding the belly fur. Where mentioned, the chestband shall be continuous around the chest of the hamster, except for a fine hairline break in the centre of the animal's chest. The cheek flashes shall be symmetrical on the animal and clearly defined, tapering to a point behind each ear. These flashes are usually bordered by lighter coloured crescents, which shall be clearly defined.

Albino (cdcdpp) *see also* Dark-eared albino/white and Black-eyed white

Sometimes referred to as the pale-eared albino/white, or flesh-eared albino/white.

The whole (entire) coat, including the belly fur, shall be pure white to the roots, and totally devoid of any shading or ticking.

Dirty, stained or discoloured fur will be penalized.

Eyes shall be bright, clear pink. (An albino's eyes are actually opaque, and the colour that one sees in the hamster's eyes is simply the blood in the blood vessels behind the eyes. Hence they appear pink.)

Ears shall be pink (i.e. flesh coloured), devoid of any colouring.

Angora *see* Long-haired

Banded *see* White band

Beige (bbdgdg)

The top colour of the hamster's coat shall be beige (soft, pale grey with a brownish tone). This colour shall be carried well down (approximately one-third) into the fur. The base colour of the fur shall be slate.

There shall be no ticking.

The hamster's crescents, which shall be clearly defined, and the belly fur, shall be white with the same base colour as the top coat.

The chestband and the cheek flashes shall be dark beige.

Eyes shall be black.

Ears shall be very dark beige.

Black-eyed cream (ee) *see also* Ruby-eyed cream and Red-eyed cream

The top colour of the hamster's coat shall be a rich, deep cream with a pink tinge, closely resembling the colour of 22-carat gold (Pantone®★ 156U). Apart from this slight tinge, the coat must be devoid of any shading. This cream colouring shall be carried well down into the coat to the roots.

The belly fur shall be a slightly lighter cream colour.

Neither the cheek flashes nor the chestband shall be visible.

Eyes shall be black.

Ears shall be dark grey, almost black.

Black-eyed ivory (eeLglg or eedgdg) *see also* Red-eyed ivory

The top coat shall be a pale greyish cream (Pantone®★ 2C) to the roots, totally devoid of any ticking or shading.

Any patches of white or other colours shall be heavily penalized.

Eyes shall be black.

Ears shall be very dark grey, almost black.

Black-eyed white (eeDsdsBaBa or eeWhwh)

The colour of the hamster's whole (entire) coat, including the belly fur, shall be pure white to the roots, completely devoid of any ticking or shading. Dirty, stained or discoloured fur will be penalized.

The chestband shall not be visible.

The cheek flashes shall not be visible.

Eyes shall be black.

Ears shall be pink (i.e. flesh coloured), devoid of any colour whatsoever.

Blonde (Lglgpp)

The colour of the hamster's top coat shall be creamy blonde. This colour shall be carried well down into the fur (approximately one-third). Ticking shall be totally absent.

The fur shall have a base colour of light grey.

The crescents, which shall be clearly defined, and the belly fur, shall be ivory.

The chestband shall be creamy blonde.

The cheek flashes shall be a darker shade of creamy blonde.

Eyes shall be claret red.

Ears shall be flesh grey.

NOTE: this variety tends to have an orange-tinted muzzle.

Cinnamon (pp)

Pantone®★ 158/159C.

The top colour of the hamster's coat shall be a rich russet orange, carried well down into the fur (approximately one-third), and completely devoid of any ticking.

The base of the fur shall be a uniform and even slate-blue colour.

The crescents (which shall be clearly defined) and the belly fur shall be ivory.

The chestband shall be a rich russet orange.

The cheek flashes shall be brown.

Eyes shall be bright claret red.

Ears shall be flesh brown.

Cinnamon fawn (pppupu)

Pantone®★ 162C.

The top colour of the hamster's coat shall be a pastel shade of orange, completely free from any shading whatsoever. This colour shall be carried well down into the fur (approximately one-third).

The base of the fur shall be a uniform and even light-grey colour.

The crescents, which shall be clearly defined, and the belly fur shall be a light-cream colour, as light as possible but not white.

The chestband shall be a pastel shade of orange, and the cheek flashes pale grey.

Eyes shall be bright, clear pink, as in the albino.

Ears shall be flesh.

NOTE: adult males of this variety are almost always infertile.

Copper (UUeebbpp)

The top coat (including belly fur) shall be a rich, clear copper to the roots.
Any patches or areas of other colour(s) shall be heavily penalized.
Eyes shall be garnet red.
Ears shall be copper grey.

Cream *see* Black-eyed cream, Red-eyed cream, and Ruby-eyed cream.

Dark-eared albino/white (cdcd) *see also* Black-eyed white, Albino

The colour of the hamster's entire coat, including the belly fur, shall be pure white to the roots, completely devoid of any ticking or shading. Dirty, stained or discoloured fur will be penalized.
The chestband shall not be visible.
The cheek flashes shall not be visible.
Eyes shall be red, approaching claret red in older animals.
Ears shall be dark grey, almost black.

Dark golden (++ Wild-type agouti)

The top colour of the hamster's coat shall be a rich and dark mahogany red, heavily ticked with black guard hairs. This colour shall be carried well down into the fur (approximately one-third).
The base of the fur shall be a uniform and even dark slate-grey colour.
The hamster's dorsal line and the top of its head, between its ears, shall be intensely ticked with dark hairs. Its face shall also have intense ticking, giving it a swarthy look with black eye rings.
The crescents, which shall be clearly defined, and the belly fur shall be a light-cream colour, as light as possible but not white.
The chestband shall be a rich, dark mahogany red.
The cheek flashes shall be black.
Eyes shall be black.
Ears shall be black.

Dark grey (dgdg)

The top colour of the hamster's coat shall be pearly grey (carried approximately one-quarter down the hairs), heavily and evenly ticked with black guard hairs (shaded as for the dark golden).
The base of the fur shall be a uniform and even dark slate grey.
The crescents, which shall be clearly defined, and the belly fur shall be as light as possible but not white.

The chestband shall be very dark slate.
The cheek flashes shall be black.
Eyes shall be black.
Ears shall be very dark grey, approaching black.

Dominant spot *see* Piebald

Fawn *see* Ruby-eyed fawn

Flesh-eared albino *see* Albino

Golden *see* Dark golden, Light golden, Normal golden, Guinea gold, Rust

Grey *see* Dark grey, Light grey

Guinea gold (bb)

Often referred to as Rust.
The hamster's top coat shall be a rich orange brown in colour
(Pantone®★ 138U), completely devoid of any shading or ticking.
   The base colour shall be a light slate grey.
The belly fur and crescents shall be a creamy-ivory colour.
The chestband shall be the same colour as the top coat.
Eyelids shall be light brown in colour.
Eyes shall be almost black.
Ears shall be dark grey with a hint of browny pink.

Honey (male – ppTo–; female – ppToTo)

Pantone®★ 157C.
The hamster's top coat shall be light cinnamon orange to the roots,
   and completely devoid of any shading or ticking.
The crescents, which shall be clearly defined, and the belly fur shall be
   very pale, almost whte.
The chestband shall be a light cinnamon orange.
The cheek flashes shall be cinnamon.
Eyes shall be claret red.
Ears shall be flesh grey.

Ivory *see* Black-eyed ivory and Red-eyed ivory

Light golden (++Wild-type agouti)

The top colour of the hamster's coat shall be a light fawny golden brown, devoid of any shading.

This colouring shall be carried well down into the coat (approximately one-third), and there shall be a slate-grey colouring at the base of the hairs.

The crescents, which shall be clearly defined, and the belly fur shall be a light-cream colour, as light as possible but not white.

The chestband shall be light fawny gold.

The cheek flashes shall be almost black.

Eyes shall be black.

Ears shall be grey.

Light grey (LgLg)

Pantone®★ 155C.

The top colour of the hamster's coat shall be a buttermilk colour (carried approximately one-third down the hairs), heavily and evenly ticked with almost black guard hairs (shaded as for the dark golden). The base of the fur shall be a uniform and even slate blue.

The crescents, which shall be clearly defined, and the belly fur shall be light buttermilk.

The chestband shall be slate blue.

The cheek flashes shall be extremely dark, almost black.

Eyes shall be black.

Ears shall be very dark grey, approaching black.

NOTE: this colour uses a lethal dominant gene.

Lilac (dgdgpp)

The top colour of the hamster's coat shall be lilac (Pantone®★ 406C), completely free from any shading or ticking. The base colour shall be a soft, pale grey (Pantone®★ 407C).

The belly fur and crescents shall be lilac white.

The chestband shall be the same colour as the animal's top, i.e. lilac (Pantone®★ 406C).

The cheek flashes shall be the same colour as the undercoat, i.e. a warm grey (Pantone®★ 407C).

Eyes shall be claret red.

Ears shall be a pinkish grey.

★Pantone, Inc.'s check–standard trademark for color.

Long-haired

Often referred to as Angora.

The colour and markings of all long-haired hamsters shall be as defined for that colour standard, allowances being made for the diluting effect of this coat type.

The coat shall be as long as possible, and soft and silky. Matting, or signs of such matting being cut/pulled out, shall be heavily penalized.

Allowance must be made for sexual dimorphism in the length of the coat, i.e. the male hamster will always have longer fur than the female. Males with shorter hair will be penalized, and females with longer hair will be penalized.

Eye colour shall be as stipulated for the full-colour variety.

Ear colour shall be as stipulated for the full-colour variety.

Melanistic black (aa) *see also* Sable

Introduced to the UK in 1990.

The hamster's whole (entire) coat shall be black, including the belly fur. The colouring shall be solid and even, without any shading, and shall be carried to the roots. No circles of lighter coloured fur around the eyes are permissible; if they are present, they shall be heavily penalized. White 'socks' are permissible and shall *not* be penalized.

Eyes shall be black.

Ears shall be black.

Normal golden (++ Wild-type agouti)

The top colour of the hamster's coat shall be a rich, deep chestnut, lightly and evenly ticked with mahogany. This colouring shall be carried well down into the coat (approximately one-third), and there shall be a dark slate-grey colouring at the base of the hairs.

The crescents, which shall be clearly defined, and the belly fur shall be a light-cream colour, almost but not quite white.

The chestband shall be bright chestnut.

The cheek flashes shall be almost black.

Eyes shall be black.

Ears shall be very dark grey, approaching black.

Pale-eared albino *see* Albino

Pearl *see* Smoke pearl

Piebald

Includes dominant spot.

The piebald or dominant spot variety of hamster shall have the appearance of a coloured animal with white spots. These markings shall be clearly defined and evenly distributed over the animal's coat. There shall be even amounts of white and colour. All white areas shall be white to the roots.

Eye colour shall be as stipulated for the full-colour variety; red or ruby-red eyes are also permissible.

Ear colour shall be as stipulated for the full-colour variety; patches of flesh colouring, or entirely flesh-coloured ears, are also permissible.

Pink-eared albino *see* Albino

Red-eyed cream (eepp)

The entire top coat shall be a deep, rich cream (Pantone 149u) to the roots, completely devoid of any ticking or shading.

Eyes shall be claret red.

Ears shall be peach grey.

Red-eyed ivory (eeLglgpp or eedgdgpp) *see also* Black-eyed ivory

The top coat shall be a pale greyish cream (Pantone 2c) to the roots, totally devoid of any shading or ticking.

Any patches of white or other colour shall be heavily penalized.

Eyes shall be garnet red.

Ears shall be pinkish grey.

Rex-coated

Sometimes referred to as rex or rexoid.

The colour and markings of a rex-coated hamster shall be exactly as that for the full-colour standard variety, with allowances made for the diluting effect of this coat type.

The coat shall be dense and soft, with a proliferation of waving. Breaks in the fur caused by the hamster moving shall not be penalized.

The whiskers shall be curly.

Eye colour shall be as stipulated for the full-colour variety.

Ear colour shall be as stipulated for the full-colour variety.

Roan (eeUUWhwh or aaWhwh or eeUUDsds) *see also* Piebald

The top coat shall be white to the roots, heavily and evenly ticked
  with black, giving an even distribution of colour. Patches of white
  or insufficient ticking shall be penalized.
Eyes shall be black.
Ears shall be dark grey, almost black. Flesh-coloured patches are
  acceptable and shall *not* be penalized.

Ruby-eyed cream (eeruru)

The hamster's top coat, including the belly fur, shall be a warm pastel
  cream, totally devoid of any shading. This cream colouring shall be
  carried to the roots.
The cheek flashes shall not be visible.
Eyes shall be ruby red.
Ears shall be pink (i.e. flesh coloured), devoid of any colour
  whatsoever.

Ruby-eyed fawn (ruru)

The top colour of the hamster's coat shall be a clear, bright fawn
  (Pantone 138u/472u), completely devoid of any shading or ticking.
  This colouring shall be carried well down into the coat, and the base
  colour shall be a light slate grey.
The belly fur and the crescent shall be almost (but not quite) white.
The chestband and cheek flashes shall be fawn.
Eyes shall be ruby red.
Ears shall be pale grey.

Rust (bb) *see* Guinea gold

Sable (UUee)

Previously known in the UK, prior to 1990, as black.
The top coat shall be black, with this colouring carried well down into
  the fur. Fine ivory-grey circles shall be present around both eyes.
The base colour shall be ivory grey.
Apart from the eye circles (which are permissible and which shall *not*
  be penalized), there shall be no other patches or areas of colour other
  than black showing on the top coat. Any such areas or patches will
  be heavily penalized.
Eyes shall be black.
Ears shall be black.

Satin

The colour and markings of a satin-coated hamster shall be exactly as
that for the full-colour standard variety, with allowances made for
the effect of this coat type, i.e. satinization deepens the colourings.

The coat shall be dense, soft, and extremely glossy, giving the animal
a satin sheen.

Eye colour shall be as stipulated for the full-colour variety.

Ear colour shall be as stipulated for the full-colour variety.

Sepia

There is no specific genotype for sepia, as the colour is produced by
selectively breeding goldens.

The top colour of the hamster's coat shall be a light tawny beige. This
colouring shall be carried well down into the coat, and the base
colour shall be a pale grey.

The top coat shall have a fine shading of dark guard hairs, and this
shading must be even over the entire top and sides of the animal.
Any unevenness in shading, and/or any light-coloured patches, will
be penalized.

The belly fur and the crescents shall be almost white.

The chestband shall be a light tawny beige.

The cheek flashes shall be almost black, made up of concentrated
ticking.

Eyes shall be black.

Ears shall be dark grey.

Silver grey (Sg)

The top colour of the hamster's coat shall be light grey, with a dark
grey undercoat. The entire coat shall be heavily and evenly ticked
with black guard hairs.

The belly fur and crescent shall be as light as possible, almost white.

The chestband shall be dark grey.

The cheek flashes shall be as dark as possible, almost black, consisting
of concentrated ticking.

Eyes shall be black.

Ears shall be black.

Smoke pearl (female – dgdgToTo; male – dgdgTo)

The top colour of the hamster's coat shall be a pale greyish cream
(Pantone 2c), and this colouring shall be carried down to the roots.
The entire coat shall be heavily and evenly ticked with black guard
hairs.

The belly fur and crescent shall be almost white.

The chestband shall be the same colour as the top coat.

The cheek flashes shall be as dark as possible, almost black, consisting of concentrated ticking.

Eyes shall be black.

Ears shall be dark grey, almost black.

Tortoiseshell and white

The colour of the hamster's coat shall consist of equal amounts of a standard colour, plus yellow and white, evenly distributed to give a balanced (i.e. symmetrical) pattern. All of these patches must be clearly defined. Heavy brindling will be penalized.

All colours must conform to those stipulated for the full-colour variety.

Eye colour shall be as stipulated for the full-colour variety.

Ear colour shall be as stipulated for the full-colour variety.

White *see* Albino, Dark-eared albino, Black-eyed white

White band

Sometimes simply referred to as banded.

The colour of the hamster's coat shall consist of that specified for the full-colour variety, plus a white band completely traversing the width of the hamster's back, midway along its body. All colours must conform to those stipulated for the full-colour variety.

The white band shall be one-third of the hamster's body length, and be unbroken. The whole of the band shall be clear, distinct and sharply defined. The edges of the band shall be parallel.

Eye colour shall be as stipulated for the full-colour variety.

Ear colour shall be as stipulated for the full-colour variety; patches of flesh-colouring or entirely flesh-coloured ears are also permissible.

White bellied

The top colour and the base colour of the animal shall be the same as that of the 'normal' standard, except that a sprinkling of white hairs will be present, having the effect of diluting the colour. This effect must be allowed for by the judge and no penalties shall be incurred for these white hairs.

The belly fur shall be pure white to the roots. The line of demarcation shall be straight, encircling the whole of the hamster's body in such a way that the whole of the underneath of the hamster (including legs and feet but not the tail) shall be white.

Eyes shall be as for the standard colour.

Ears shall be as for the standard colour.

THE SHOW

Show pens

All exhibits at a hamster show (except pet hamsters) have to be benched in a standard show pen. This is so that the judge can have no idea who owns any particular hamster, thus ensuring his impartiality. These show pens can be bought or made. You will need about 12–20 of these if you keep a fair number of hamsters for showing. They need not, of course, all be purchased at the same time.

If you are intending building these show pens yourself, here is the U.K. standard. By reading about it and studying the photograph opposite or, better still, an actual show pen, all will become apparent and construction will be seen to be reasonably easy.

The body of the standard show pen shall be made from 9mm (⅜in) plywood, with the ends of 6mm (¼in) plywood. The wire front and fitting shall be made from 16SWG wire, with tin endings.

The external measurements of the pen shall be 204mm (8in) long, 153mm (4in) high, and 153mm (4in) deep. The wooden top shall extend 63mm (2½in) from the back of the outside edge of the pen, and the wooden front shall extend 45mm (1¾in) from the outside edge of the bottom of the pen. The open edges of both the wooden top and front shall be edged with tin.

The wire front shall consist of 20 vertical pieces of 16SWG wire, each 160mm (6¼in) long, and braced with four crossbars of flat tin, 4mm (⅝in) wide by 1mm (1/32in) and 187mm (7⅜in) long. These crossbars must be punched (4.5mm or 3/16in centre to centre), and shall be fixed across both the top and bottom of the wire front. One crossbar shall also be fixed 63mm (2½in) from the top and one crossbar fixed 45mm (1¾in) from the bottom of the wire front. The entire wire front shall be bent through a right angle on a 12.5mm (½in) radius exactly central between the two middle crossbars. The entire wire front shall be hinged 6mm (¼in) from the top of the wooden front. The ninth vertical bar from the left shall be continued and bent over to form the ninth vertical bar from the right. In so doing, the bend of this wire shall form a fastening loop, extending 45mm (1¾in) from the top of the wire front. This loop is part of the wire front.

A golden hamster in a standard show pen.

In the centre of the top wooden piece, a semi-circular handle (63mm or 2½in in diameter) shall be fitted, held in place by two wire staples, fixed through the 10mm (⅜in) circles on each end of this handle. The two eyelets shall be placed 50mm (2in) from the outside edge of the back of the cage, and 70mm (2¾in) from the outside edge of the side of the pen. All wire ends shall be cut off and flattened inside the pen, so as not to cause injury to any hamster placed in the pen.

A piece of 16SWG wire shall be fixed in the centre of the two staples. The end of this wire shall be formed into a complete circle (10mm or ⅜in in diameter), and the whole of this fastener shall be so fixed as to allow it to be rotated through 360°, thereby acting as a fastener for the show pen, in conjunction with the loop that is an integral part of the wire front.

The whole of the outside of the wooden part of the pen, the fastener and the carrying handle shall be painted with a high gloss, non-toxic black paint. The whole of the inside of the wooden parts of the pen, the tin edging and the whole of the cage front (including the loop) shall be painted with a high gloss, non-toxic white paint.

No food or bedding shall be left in the show pen when it is benched.

The floor shall be covered by a thin layer of sawdust or shavings, except in the case of long-haired hamsters, when cat litter (of any material) must be used.

The only identifying marks allowed on a show pen are the owner's name and address, which must be placed on the bottom of the pen.

Choosing stock for a show

You should carry out your own mini show, in order to decide which of your hamsters are the best and are, therefore, the ones which you should enter in the real show. Ensure that they are complete (i.e. no missing limbs, eyes, etc.), clean and in good condition. If you are showing white hamsters, then they will probably benefit from a bath a couple of days before the show. Use a mild shampoo – one designed for babies is suitable. Place about 30–40mm (1–1½in) of lukewarm water in a bowl, and gently place the hamster in it. Gently rub the hamster with the water, and then apply a small amount of shampoo. This should be rubbed in well, paying particular attention to any soiled areas on the hamster's fur. When you have covered all of the animal, avoiding its eyes, ears, mouth and nose, thoroughly rinse off the shampoo. The hamster must now be dried, before being placed back in its freshly cleaned cage. The cage should then be left in a warm area overnight, well away from any draughts.

Rubbing a hamster's fur with a silk handkerchief will help to give it a good sheen on its coat. This treatment must be carried out on a regular (i.e. daily) basis for 10–14 days prior to the show, if your actions are to have any marked advantageous effect.

Long-haired hamsters need to be groomed daily, and even more often before a show. An old, clean toothbrush is ideal for this purpose. If you discover some matted hair, you should not try to cut it out, as this will result in your losing points at the show. Instead, gently tease it out with your fingers and the toothbrush or an old fine-toothed comb.

Transport of entries

If you are going to the show in person, your entries should be transported in separate carrying boxes, *not* their show pens. Regular transport of hamsters in show pens will result in the pens becoming soiled; the hamsters will also gnaw on the bars and interiors of the cages. This will mean that, at the very least, you will need to paint the show pens much more often than would otherwise be necessary and, at the worst, you will have to repair or replace the pens due to the damage done to them by the hamsters' teeth.

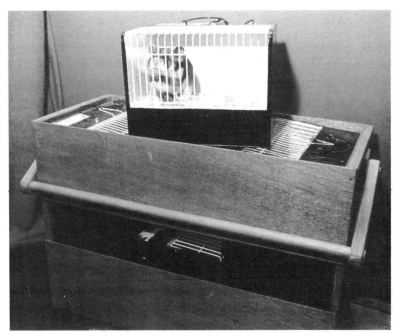

Six show pens in a transporter, about to be taken to a show.

If you transport your stock in separate boxes, you can safely place plenty of bedding in those boxes. This will have the effect of grooming your hamsters as they push their way through the bedding.

If you are sending your stock by rail, you can either hire a show pen from the show secretary and transport your stock in a plain box, or you can construct a travelling box large enough to carry the required number of show pens and strong enough to survive any rough handling that it may get on its travels. Ensure that you have sufficient ventilation holes in the carry box, and place several 'livestock' stickers on the outside of the box. These stickers are available from most railway goods depots.

Ensure that the show secretary knows that you are sending stock by rail, and that you are both aware of when the stock should be returned to you. Many rail depots close for parcels over the weekend, and so you may have to send them on a Friday and have them returned to you on the following Monday, if the show is held on a Saturday.

Any food that you place in the show pens must be easily removed, and a dog biscuit along with a piece of apple, turnip or some other such item will supply food and moisture during the hamster's travels. Never place carrots or other strongly coloured foods with light or white hamsters, as the hamsters will become stained.

Entering a show

In order to get the most out of your hamstering, you should join at least one hamster club. This will also enable you to obtain details of all shows in your area. As a member, you will receive a show schedule, giving full details of every forthcoming show: the venue, the show officials, the various classes, prizes and an entry form.

You should carefully read the schedule and decide in which classes you wish to enter your stock. Most shows have classes for novices (limited to those who have never won a first prize before), straight classes (into which you must enter each hamster before you can enter it into any more classes at that show), duplicate classes (into which you can enter your hamsters – provided that they have qualified in a relevant straight class), and a pet-hamster class.

Guidelines for U.K. show entries

Class	Limitations
Novice	Owner (*not* hamster) must not have won a first prize before.
Junior Male	A male hamster belonging to a club member aged 16 years or under.
Junior Female	A female hamster belonging to a club member aged 16 years or under.
Duplicate Class	Must first be entered in the straight class (i.e. the class specifically for that variety).
Breeder's	Exhibit must have been bred by exhibitor.
Sportsman's	Reversed prize money given.
Supporter's	No prize money given.
Grand Challenge	Open to any animal entered in a straight class. It is not necessary for a hamster to be entered in this class to win the Best in Show or Best Opposite Sex awards.

The entry form should be filled in and sent – together with a cheque to cover the total entry fees and fees for the hire of show pens if relevant – to the show secretary. Enclose a self-addressed and stamped envelope with your entries to allow the show secretary to return the show pen labels to you without the club incurring postage costs which it cannot afford.

The name of the variety exhibited must be written on each show pen label, and placed in the top left-hand corner of the wooden top piece of the show pen. You must then make a record of which hamster is to be placed in which show pen.

On arrival

When you arrive at the show, tell the show secretary that you are there, and then place all your entries, in their respective show pens, on the benches, where the stock will wait until it is judged. This is referred to as 'benching the entries'. From this point, only certain show officials (the judge, the pen stewards and the book steward) may handle any pen or exhibit that has been benched. This is true until the show secretary has been informed by the judge that the judging is over. The show secretary must then inform the exhibitors.

Show officials

The judge, book steward and pen stewards should all wear white coats, which helps other exhibitors to see at a glance whether or not a person handling an exhibit is an authorized official.

The duties of the different officials in the U.K. (all volunteers) are given below. These may vary from time to time and from one country to the next.

Show secretary

This person must book a suitable hall (in consultation with the club's show manager) for the show; record all entries; issue all show pen labels; account for all entry monies; issue prize cards (correctly filled in); organize the refreshments; organize the raffle and/or any other fund-raising events on the day; arrange local publicity (in conjunction with the club's P.R.O.); issue a list of prize winners; and publish a full report of the show in relevant journals.

A show secretary and her assistant organize the prize cards and record the results at a show.

The show manager checks that all of the trophies are present and correct.

Show manager

This person has overall charge of all aspects of the show and, should there be a disagreement, he must adjudicate. It is his job to plan the whole series of shows throughout the year, order show stationery (such as prize cards, judging sheets, etc.).

Trophy manager

This person must allocate trophies to all classes at all shows, ensuring that they are clean and in good repair. It is his responsibility to ensure that all trophies are signed for, and that a record is kept of their whereabouts. He must also remind former winners of when they must return their trophies, for them to be issued again.

Pen steward

There are usually several pen stewards at each show. They must place all of the show pens and exhibits on the judge's table at the appropriate time, and fetch and carry them as the judge wishes.

Book steward

The book steward sits at the side of the judge, noting his comments and recording the points that are given to each entry.

Hamsters in the Any Other Colour (standard) class await their turn on the judging bench.

Judge

The judge is in total charge of the judging of all entries and his decision is final. Many judges have 20 or more years of experience under their belts. The highest grade of judge in the U.K. is the N.S.H.C. Recognized Judge, of whom there are only a few.

During the show

Do not waste time during the show while your hamsters are being judged. Use it wisely to discuss all aspects of hamsters with other breeders present at the show. You may be able to get the answer to one of your own problems, obtain new stock, sell some of your surplus stock, discuss the suitability of a certain variety or a dozen other things. Only at a show will you find so many experienced breeders/exhibitors under one roof, and all with a wealth of experience and knowledge that they will gladly share with you.

After the show

When the judging is completed and the show secretary has announced that you may now recover your entries, you should do so, and then place them in their travel boxes ready for their trip home. Shortly after completion of judging, there will be the prize-giving ceremony, after which the show will be officially declared closed.

Some judges will give individual reports on each and every hamster entered at a particular show; indeed, in some clubs this is mandatory. These reports will act as a guide to you to see where your stock is failing, and also the good points that it possesses. If you still wish to find out more, take your hamster, along with its report, to the judge and ask for more details. Even in those clubs where such individual reports are not mandatory, I would recommend that all judges use the system. True, it does take a little more time and effort but, to my mind, the advantages (especially to the tyro) far outweigh the disadvantages.

In almost every club, it is part of the judge's duties to send a full Show Report to the Fancy's own journal, and this should contain enough details (at least on those hamsters who have been successful at the show) to indicate why they have been so successful. This kind of report does not, however, help breeders as much as the individual reports do.

When you arrive home, before you do anything else, ensure that all of your hamsters are returned to their own cages, fed and properly seen to. You can then treat yourself to a cup of tea, while you mull over the happenings of the day.

CHAPTER 8

Judging

If you are really bitten by the hamstering bug, you will probably eventually aspire to be a judge. However, before you can do this, you will have to gain experience of all of the other jobs concerned with hamster shows. Most good clubs insist that, before anyone can be considered for training as a judge, the person must carry out the duties of pen steward and book steward at several different shows and under the guidance of several different judges.

The pen stewards are the hard-working people whose job it is to arrange all the entries on the judging benches, ensuring that all the relevant entries are given to the judge at the appropriate time. This may sound easy and even mundane, but a couple of really good pen stewards, who know exactly what they are doing, can make life so much easier for a judge at any show.

The book steward is the person who sits next to the judge, noting and recording his comments, and recording the number of points awarded to each entry under each category. As a book steward, you will learn much about the art of judging, and pick up many tricks of the trade. Some clubs use this position to train would-be judges; others run specific training courses.

Once you have carried out these duties and, in the eyes of the club's show manager and executive committee, gained sufficient experience, you will be appointed a trainee judge. At this stage, you will only be allowed to judge shows while under the direct supervision of nominated experienced judges. All of these judges will be noting your performance and offering guidance as and when needed. They will also have to write a detailed report concerning your efforts and your suitability (or otherwise) as a judge. When several judges have assessed your performance and reported favourably to the show manager, you will be appointed as a club judge. In the U.K., after several years (or even longer!) as a club judge, you may again be assessed, this time by senior National Syrian Hamster Council Recognized Judges. If they report favourably on your performance, you too may become an N.S.H.C. Recognized Judge – the highest accolade given to any hamster fancier.

A judge's kit, packed safely into a sturdy carrying box, to ensure that all items are always to hand.

EQUIPMENT

Certain pieces of equipment are necessary if the judge is to do his job to the best of his ability. While some people would argue that not all of the following is essential all of the time, if you make it a habit always to carry all of the kit whenever you are officiating as a judge at a show, you will soon learn the advantages, as you will be covered for almost every eventuality that you are likely to meet. It is not, however, the last word in judging equipment; every experienced judge will add items to, or subtract items from, this list.

1. Judging board

This is a wooden or metal frame, covered with wire mesh, on which the hamster is judged. It is of a size to fit easily into a standard show pen, enabling the hamster to be scooped out. This is particularly important if the hamster has just awakened from a deep sleep and is not feeling totally at peace with the world!

The hamster is placed on the judging board and, by turning the board, the hamster can be studied without any stress. By placing a hand over the hamster's back, it is possible to turn the animal on is back, which will enable it to be sexed, and the colour and markings of

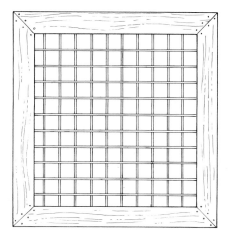

Fig. 21 Judging board or frame, an essential for every serious hamster fancier. Simply made from timber and welded mesh, its dimensions should be such that it will fit inside a standard show pen, enabling you to scoop out the hamster inside. This frame has many uses for the hamster keeper, from examining the animal to breaking up fighting hamsters in the mating cage.

its belly fur to be examined. Although at first the board will seem a clumsy way of handling the hamsters, experience will soon prove otherwise. The board must be thoroughly cleaned and disinfected between each hamster judged and after each show, in order to reduce the risk of infection amongst the exhibited hamsters.

2. Adjustable reading lamp

When fitted with a 'daylight' bulb, this device will enable the true colours of all the exhibits to be seen. Its use will also ensure that all hamsters are judged under the same light source throughout the day. Many clubs insist on its use wherever possible. Don't forget to take a spare bulb!

3. Electric extension cable

This will enable the lamp to be used when the nearest electric socket is some distance away. A 10-m (10-yd) cable is ideal, although a 5-m (5-yd) cable is usually sufficient. Be very careful about the cable, ensuring that it will not be positioned where it can trip any one, causing injury. If you need to pass it over a walkway, tape it securely to the floor, and check it at regular intervals during the day.

4. Judging notebook

This should be a loose-leaf-type book (either A4 or A5 size), containing all details of every recognized standard. These standards are merely copied from the club handbook into this notebook, one standard per page. I also like to write my own comments, observations and notes concerning each variety. For example, I note the common faults, any sexual dimorphism that is likely to be seen in that variety, and so on. Only experience will tell you these but, when talking to experienced judges and/or breeders, you will come across lots of such interesting items, and they should all be noted for future reference. A loose-leaf book will enable all standards to be kept in strict alphabetical order, new ones added when accepted, and old ones removed or amended. A series of dividers, labelled alphabetically, will be indispensable for ease of use of this book.

I also cross-reference all standards, to enable me to find all possible alternatives and thereby arrive at the correct standard. For example, under 'white', my book points me to the standards for dark-eared albino, black-eyed white, and pale-eared albino.

5. PANTONE Color Formula Guide 1000

This is an international colour guide which enables any specified colour to be found, still maintaining the exact colour and shade. They have not yet received the blessing and endorsement of every hamster club, but can be used to indicate the colours of various standards. They are quite expensive to buy, but judges should acquire a copy, using it to guide themselves and other fanciers as to the specific colours required in standards.

6. First aid kit

This is necessary for both human and animal injuries (see Chapter 9, Ailments). It is essential for when you find an injured hamster in a show, or when a particularly bad-tempered hamster decides to exact revenge on the fingers that have just aroused it from a deep sleep!

7. Paper tissues

For cleaning the judging frame and lots of other such jobs, paper tissues are invaluable. Moist tissues are also handy to have.

8. Disinfectant spray

For 'sterilizing' the hands and the judging board after handling a hamster suspected of having a contagious disease. Some clubs insist on

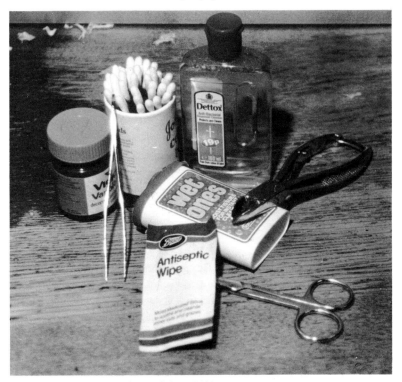

The minimum contents of a small first aid kit.

its use to clean the judging board between *every* hamster – a course of action which I strongly recommend.

9. Coloured stickers

These are for placing on the show pens (on the label) when a class has been judged. They are usually rectangular or square in shape, although some judges prefer star-shaped stickers. The convention is that a red sticker indicates a first-prize winner, a blue the second, a yellow the third, and a green sticker the 'reserve' (fourth). 'Very highly commended' (fifth), 'highly commended' (sixth), and 'commended' (seventh) do not receive any coloured sticker.

Plain white or fluorescent orange stickers are also useful for writing notes on ('Please see judge' etc.) and placing on the cage. This is especially useful when you discover something like an injury, which needs drawing to the attention of the owner.

10. Red pen (indelible ink)

For writing the total number of points on an entry's pen label.

11. Judging sheets

These are A4-sized sheets that are pre-marked into columns with headings related to points allocation (e.g. 'colour and markings', 'type' etc.). The following is my own preferred layout for these sheets, but other judges may have other ideas.

Suggested layout of judging sheet

Pen no.	Colour and markings	Type	Fur	Size	Condition	Eyes and ears	Sex	Comments	Total points

---

12. Magnifying glass

Although very rarely used on the judging bench, this can be handy to check whether a chestband is closed (bad) or has a *very* fine hairline break (excellent). Also it is very useful for checking injuries, such as cuts and bites, on any hamsters.

JUDGING PROCEDURE

As detailed in an earlier chapter, in the U.K. the N.S.H.C. set down standards for the 'perfect' hamster in every recognized variety. As a judge, you must be able to picture this animal in your mind's eye; this is the hamster against which all of the hamsters at any show are judged. It is important to remember this, as the hamsters are not competing against each other for the allocation of points. If you came across a hamster which *exactly* matched this 'perfect hamster', it would be given 100 points. The chance of this happening is negligible; in over 30 years' experience, I have never come across such a hamster.

The reason that I emphasize that the hamsters are not actually competing against each other, is that, in several classes (in particular duplicate classes and A.O.C. – Any Other Colour – classes), different varieties will be in the same class and it is almost impossible to judge them against each other. What happens is that each one is judged against the 'perfect hamster' for that variety, and then the points are compared to see which is the best, i.e. the one with the highest number of points is obviously the best hamster. More details will be given on this subject later in this section.

At the beginning of the show, the show secretary will give sheets to the judge, listing all the entries in every class. The entries are given a number, e.g. the first hamster entered in class 1 will have the number 101; the third will have 103. The first hamster entered in class 3 will be given the number 301; the third, 303 etc. This number is entered in the lefthand box of the pen label and will apply for all of the 'straight' classes, into which every show hamster must be entered before it may be entered in any of the duplicate classes. The righthand side of the pen label shows in which duplicate classes the hamster is entered, and is usually titled 'also in classes'. For instance, if entry number 415 (i.e. the 15th hamster entered in class 4) is also in classes 12, 13, 14 and 15, the pen label will be as follows:

Pen label

Pen number	**Also in classes**
415	12, 13, 14, 15

The pen labels are always attached to the left-hand corner of the top of the show pen.

The pen stewards will place all the entries in class 1 on the actual judging bench (moving them from the holding benches, where their owners have placed them). The judge then takes the first entry out of its show pen, telling the book steward the number on the show pen. He then examines it thoroughly, giving the number of marks that he awards the hamster for each category.

When I do this, I like to work to a routine, so that I don't overlook any feature. I pick the hamster out of its show pen and place it on my judging board. I then briefly look at its top coat and then turn it over. Once on its back, I sex the hamster, look at its belly fur, examine any markings on the underneath, check it for cuts etc., check its nails and then turn it the right way up. This brings me to its head.

I check its teeth (for correct growth but also an indication of its age – old hamsters have yellow teeth, young hamsters have white teeth), its nose for loss of fur ('nose-rub', caused by nagging at the bars of his cage), its ears for injury and shape etc. (also an indication of its age – young hamsters have a light covering of white hairs on their ears, those of old hamsters are shiny), and then study the colour and markings on the top of the hamster in great detail.

I check for moult, injuries and deformities and then tell the book steward how many points I have awarded for each category. Any injuries, lack of alertness, hip spots showing (the glands on the flanks of all hamsters), excess fat, etc. result in a loss of marks under the

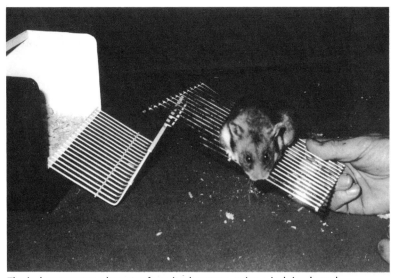

The judge removes a hamster from its show pen, using a judging board.

Condition category. Poor fur is penalized under Fur, and the Eyes and Ears category only concerns the size, shape and placing of these organs and *not* colour (which comes under the Colour and Markings category).

No fault should be penalized twice. All faults are noted in the Comments column, for future use if necessary. If a hamster is shown in a dirty, damaged or 'tatty' show pen, I make enquiries to see if it is a hire pen. If it is, I make a note to see the show manager about it later (!); if it isn't, I note it in my Comments column. I do not usually deduct points for this *except* in extreme cases or where two entries have exactly the same points. In these cases I will subtract 0.5–10 points, depending on the severity of the 'offence'.

When all of the hamsters in a class have been judged, the pen stewards will place the seven with the highest marks on the judge's bench, in descending order. If they all have different marks, life is easy and the awards are made accordingly. However, almost without exception, there is at least one pair who have exactly the same number of points. The judge then has to look at them even more closely, and both at the same time. He needs to decide if he has been consistent with his points allocation, and so almost re-judge them to decide which one is the better hamster. In a small straight class this is relatively easy, but in a duplicate class of 50+, I often find that I have several hamsters with the same marks, and this is much more difficult. There can, after all, be only one winner!

Of course, every judge will have his own methods of judging, and every judge will interpret the standards in a slightly different way, but that is all part of the pleasures of exhibiting any animal – hamsters included!

COMMON FAULTS

There are some common faults among hamsters in general, and some that are peculiar to a specific variety. Unfortunately, space does not permit me to list the latter, but some of the more common, general faults are listed below.

Common faults occurring in hamsters	
Narrow head	Bent ears
Under-/overshot jaws	Thin fur
Overgrown/broken teeth	Long fur on short-haired varieties
Damaged ears	Hip spots too prominent
Cuts and sores	Excess fat
Parasites (usually fleas etc.)	Poor and indistinct markings
Dirty fur	Poor colour
Overgrown claws (nails)	

There are times when, because of some of these faults (e.g. illness, injury, parasites, etc.), a judge will need to take drastic action. He cannot allow any animal to remain in the show if he suspects that:

a) It has an infectious or contagious disease,
b) It is in pain,
c) It has ectoparasites.

In such cases, he has only one choice – the animal must be disqualified, and the owner must immediately be informed of the reason and advised to remove the animal from the show venue and, if necessary, seek veterinary advice and treatment for the hamster.

The judge's decision is always final, and no one should argue, although most judges are quite happy to discuss the performance of a specific entry *after* the show, over a well-deserved cup of coffee. Likewise, if the judge has to disqualify any hamster, he should do it in a quiet manner which will not embarrass the owner unduly.

The judge's job is not easy, and to do it well requires a great amount of experience, hard work and dedication. Judges, in common with all other hamster club officials, do not get paid for their labours; on the contrary, the judge will probably incur a great deal of expense in travelling to the show, purchasing his equipment etc. It is also worth remembering that all judges are human and will, at some time in their career, make a mistake or two. Good judges will own up to this, learn from their mistakes and go on to be even better judges.

If you have aspirations to become a judge yourself, you should seek as much help as possible from experienced judges. Some clubs run training sessions; others allow would-be trainees to sit near to the judge during a show, with the judge commenting out loud and explaining just what he is looking for. Experience is the prime requisite and can, of course, only be gained and not learned.

CHAPTER 9

Ailments

Hamsters are, on the whole, less susceptible to disease and illness than many other animals, provided that they are kept in good conditions and fed a well-balanced diet. If you suspect that any of your hamsters is ill, do not hesitate to take it to a qualified veterinary surgeon as soon as possible. Some diseases are easily cured if prompt medical attention is sought, while the same disease may well prove fatal if the hamster is not treated early in the illness.

Prevention is, of course, better than cure. Ensure that your hamsters are:

a) Given a good, balanced diet,
b) Kept in cages which are cleaned regularly,
c) Not subjected to extremes of temperatures,
d) Kept away from draughts,
e) Are not stressed,
f) Are not allowed to climb in areas where they may fall, thus injuring themselves.

Any cuts, abrasions or bites must be cleaned and treated immediately.

FIRST AID KIT

A small first aid kit should be kept in your hamstery, and should contain the following items.

1. Nail clippers

These should be of top quality, and can be used for trimming both nails (claws) and teeth.

2. Tweezers

For the removal of foreign bodies, a pair of fine tweezers should be used.

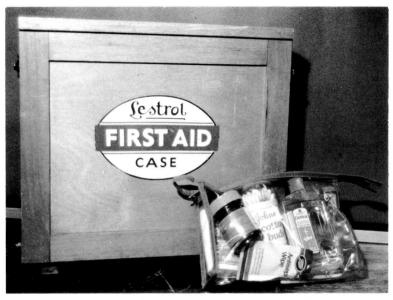

A first aid kit should be included in every hamstery. This is useful for both hamster and human injuries!

3. Scissors

These should be curved and round-ended, and are to be used to cut off the fur around the wound. They must *not* be used for trimming nails or teeth.

4. Antiseptic lotion

This is essential for cleansing cuts, wounds and abrasions.

5. Antibiotic powder

This should be applied to wounds after they have been thoroughly cleansed. This powder is only available from a veterinary surgeon, who will only supply it after he has seen the wound in question.

6. Antihistamine lotion

Occasionally, a hamster will be stung by a bee, wasp or other such insect which has managed to find its way into the hamster's cage. The sting should be removed and antihistamine lotion applied.

7. Cotton wool

For cleaning wounds, cuts and abrasions, and for stemming the flow of blood, cotton wool is indispensible.

8. Surgical gauze

A supply of gauze should be kept for padding wounds and stemming the flow of blood.

9. Adhesive plasters

Although these will soon be chewed off by the hamster, they are useful for applying directly to small wounds and for keeping dressings in place. They can also be used for minor splinting.

10. Bandages

A selection of small bandages should be kept for binding broken limbs and wounds. They will, of course, be temporary, as the hamster will chew them off.

11. Cotton buds

Ideal for cleaning wounds and the application of ointments etc. With care, they can also be used to clean the pinnae (ear flaps) but *under no circumstances* should you poke these (or any other object) down the ear canal.

12. Table salt

A solution of table salt (2 tablespoonsful of salt to ½l/1pt of water) is a good solution to wash debris from wounds and counter infection.

13. Mild disinfectant

This is useful for washing areas around wounds, in order to prevent further influx of debris. It is also recommended for washing one's own hands with, after handling any animal. Use with a spray for cleaning judging boards and cages.

14. Sodium bicarbonate

On a wet compress, this will help reduce swelling.

COMMON INJURIES AND DISEASES

As mentioned at the beginning of this chapter, the hamster is, on the whole, a healthy animal suffering from very few ailments. Most of these cannot, of course, be treated by the lay person and so must be referred to a qualified veterinary surgeon. However, it is useful for the serious fancier to know the symptoms of the most common diseases that his hamsters may contract, and so I detail them here.

Abscesses

Abscesses are simply wounds that have filled with pus, and are usually the results of fighting, especially when the wound has either been overlooked or not properly cleaned. All bites, cuts and wounds should be cleaned and disinfected to avoid the development of abscesses. Once they have developed, however, abscesses will require lancing and draining (often several times). The animals may also require a course of antibiotics (see p.164), to counter the infection. These can only be given by a qualified veterinary surgeon.

Broken limbs

Usually the result of a fall, all suspected broken limbs must be referred to a veterinary surgeon. Do not be surprised if the limb is not wrapped up or put in splints, as hamsters are notorious for chewing off such coverings. Most fractures in hamsters heal on their own with no problems.

Cage paralysis (*see also* Constipation, Dystocia, Falls, Hind limb paralysis)

This disorder is caused by keeping hamsters in cages that are too small, so that the animals do not get sufficient exercise. The condition manifests itself by the hamster dragging its back end around, appearing semi-crippled.

The cure is simple – a bigger cage and more exercise. The prevention is even simpler – don't keep hamsters in small cages!

Cannibalism

This is not a disease, but a condition that may show itself in mothers of young litters, or where more than one hamster is kept in a cage. In the first case, the reasons are usually that the mother has been supplied with insufficient food so that she cannot produce enough milk to feed her litter. She will then kill the weakest, eating them to help replace the goodness that she has used in feeding the rest of the litter. Unless she is given sufficient food, this process will continue until all of the pups have been killed and eaten. Occasionally, a mother will only kill one or two pups, even though she has more than enough food. This may be due to the pups being injured or malformed, forcing the mother to kill them. In Nature, nothing is wasted and so it is only natural that the mother will then eat the dead pups.

Where two or more adult hamsters are kept in one cage, fighting will inevitably take place. When the fighting is serious, one or more parties will get injured and, in some cases, death will result. At this time, the other party will set about eating the body of its former adversary. Obviously, the body should be removed before this happens or, even better, prevent any fights to the death by observing the golden rule of hamster keeping 'one hamster – one cage'!

It is *not* true that feeding meat will result in cannibalism.

Common cold and influenza

Viral infections cannot be transmitted from human beings to hamsters, although in similar climatic conditions, both human beings and other species of animals may exhibit similar symptoms. Colds in hamsters can easily lead to pneumonia and hence to death. The infected hamster may sneeze and snuffle, have a runny nose, and a high temperature (up to 40°C).

Treatment consists of warmth and general nursing. Placing a small piece of Vick, Olbas oil, or similar near to (but out of reach of) the hamster may also help, and a small amount rubbed on the animal's chest will be beneficial. Antibiotics, available only from a veterinary surgeon, may also be administered to fight secondary infection.

If the hamster shivers and chatters, shows weight loss, and has conjunctivitis, it may be suffering from *Pasteurella pneumotropica*, an infection of the lungs. Treatment for this consists of the administration of antibiotics such as chloramphenicol, or trimethorprim/sulphadiazine or similar potentiated sulphonamide (only available from your veterinary surgeon).

Constipation

The most common cause of constipation is a blockage of the intestine. This is usually caused by supplying poor-quality man-made or fibrous bedding, or a lack of drinking water for the hamsters, especially in young stock. In severe cases, this can cause a complete prolapse. It can also be caused by lack of exercise, poor diet, pregnancy or dystocia. The symptoms are a large, swollen abdomen (often discoloured), and a large, bulging anus. Prompt treatment is required if the hamster is to be saved.

Water must always be available for all hamsters at all times. Green foods may also help prevent this condition. Never give fibrous bedding to hamsters, thereby reducing the risk. Some manufacturers now produce bedding made from natural, short fibres, which they claim is perfectly safe for hamsters and other small mammals. I have never used this material, and so cannot comment further.

Refer all cases to your veterinary surgeon as soon as possible. He will treat such cases with a water enema, and recommend the feeding of plenty of fresh fruit and vegetables.

Cuts and bites

Hamsters can easily be injured during unsuccessful matings, when it is not uncommon for a fight to develop. After any such fight, both animals must be closely and carefully examined for injuries. If a cut or bite is found, the fur around the area should be carefully cut off, using curved, round-ended scissors. In order to stop the cut fur from falling on to the wound, dip the scissors in water, keeping the cutting edges damp throughout the operation; this will make the cut fur stick to the blades.

The wound should then be thoroughly washed with saline solution, and then treated with an antibiotic liquid. A good dusting with an antibiotic wound powder will finish the job. By carrying out this action, the dangers of an infection and/or abscess will be lessened. Any large wounds which may require stitching will, of course, need to be referred to a veterinary surgeon at the earliest opportunity.

Deformed tail

Occasionally, a newly weaned pup will be seen to have a deformed tail that seems to be stuck to its back, pointing straight up into the air. In some cases, the only indication is a slight bump or kink in the tail. This is almost always a sign of hereditary disease. Such complaints are not curable, and stock thus affected must never be bred from. It is best to have all such pups, and maybe even their parents, humanely killed. In any case, extreme care must be exercised in the breeding programme to ensure that this deformity is not transmitted to more generations of hamsters. The importance of accurate record keeping cannot be over emphasized.

Dystocia

This is the condition where a female cannot expel her young. It may be caused by excess fat on the mother-to-be, a deformity in her body, or abnormally large pups. Veterinary advice must be sought as soon as possible, if mother and pups are to be saved.

Ectoparasites (*see also* Skin diseases)

Fleas and mites, transmitted from other animals and/or fouled bedding, occur on some hamsters. All such infected hamsters must be taken to a vet for positive identification of the parasite, and then the appropriate treatment administered.

Endoparasites

These are internal parasites and, in the hamster, consist of one of two types:

Dwarf tapeworms
Many hamsters are infected with these parasites, but do not usually show any symptoms. Very often the first indication of an infestation is the detection of ova in the hamster's faeces. Treatment consists of the administration of niclosamide.

Pinworm
Present in many hamsters, this parasite is thought to be harmless. Eggs of this worm are banana-shaped and, in infected hamsters, can usually be seen in the faeces. Treatment consists of thiabendazole or piperazine citrate.

Falls

Hamsters are extremely short-sighted, and so can easily fall and injure themselves if left unattended for any length of time. Bones may be broken and the hamster may be in shock.

The faller must be carefully examined and, if no serious injury is found, it can be placed back in its cage. The cage should then be placed in a warm, dark and quiet place, and the hamster checked every few hours. It is advisable to have him checked out by your vet at the earliest possible opportunity. If you suspect any broken bones, veterinary assistance must be sought immediately.

Heat stroke *see* Sleeper disease

Hibernation

Whether or not hamsters hibernate has been a topic of discussion for many years, some people arguing that the hamster is actually in a comatose state, rather than true hibernation. (Hibernation is the condition adopted by some animals to pass the winter months; this is clearly not the case with the hamster.) It is known that, when the ambient temperature drops below 5°C (41°F), the hamster's body

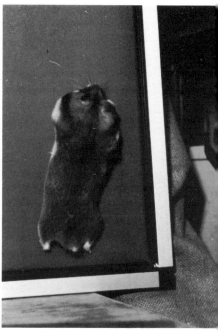

A sequence of three photographs showing that hamsters can climb. Unfortunately, due to their poor eyesight, they can easily fall, often seriously injuring or even killing themselves.

temperature will drop and its pulse and respiratory rate will slow markedly. This is often referred to as 'hibernation'. If a hamster is found in this state, it should be placed (in its cage) in a warm position and left for 30–60 minutes. No direct heat should be applied. It is often possible to revive such a hamster by gently holding it (for the same period) in the hands, until it starts to come to, at which time it should be replaced in his cage.

As with all such things, prevention is better than cure. Hamsters should not be kept in rooms or buildings where the temperature is liable to drastic and sudden changes. This is the state of affairs that exists in most living rooms or houses in general, where the central heating is on during the day and/or early evening, keeping the temperature at 20–30°C (68–86°F) but where, during the early hours of the morning when the heating is off, the temperature plummets. It is this sudden change of temperature that hamsters cannot deal with, and not the low temperatures *per se*. I have known hamsters to be kept in an unheated hamstery where the ambient temperature in the building was around 0°C (32°F) for much of the winter, causing water bottles to freeze daily. However, the hamsters were all supplied with generous quantities of bedding and, throughout the winter, not one hamster hibernated! In fact, litters were successfully bred and reared.

Keep your hamsters in even temperatures and supply plenty of good quality bedding in their cages, and you will find that they do not hibernate.

Hind limb paralysis

Incidence of a paralysis of the hind limbs of male hamsters of 6–10 months may indicate a hereditary (and sex-linked) factor. There is obviously no cure for this and affected animals (and their progeny and siblings) should not be used for breeding.

Hind limb paralysis can also be caused by other factors including small cages, falls, constipation and dystocia. Veterinary advice should be sought in all cases.

Hip spots

Hip spots are not signs of illness or disease. They are glands which are situated on the hamster's hips. Both sexes possess these but, usually, they are easily noticeable only in the male. They are particularly prominent during the summer, or on a male who is kept close to ovulating females. At such times, the male licks these hip spots, making the fur around them wet and, on some occasions, even making the area completely bald. Do not attempt to apply any ointment to the area.

As usual, if you have any reason to suspect illness, or are at all worried about the health of your hamster, consult with your vet.

Impacted cheek pouches

As the inside of a hamster's cheek pouches are dry, and not moist as in human beings, sticky foods fed to the hamster can become impacted (wedged in the pouches). This problem usually manifests itself as a 'lump' in the affected pouch and, on several occasions, this had led the owner (and some vets) to believe that the hamster had an abscess. Hamsters thought to be suffering from this condition must be taken to a vet, who will then empty the pouch and rinse it with water, to remove both debris and the stickiness that caused the problem.

As most problems of this type result from the feeding of chocolate and sweets to hamsters, prevention is, therefore, simple – do not feed sweets and chocolate to your hamsters!

Loss of fur *see* Skin diseases

Overgrown nails (claws)

Like many other pets, hamsters will often require their toe nails clipping. Ask your vet to show you how to do this before attempting the operation yourself.

Overgrown teeth

Hamsters are rodents, possessing constantly growing teeth. In normal circumstances, the teeth are worn down (by gnawing on hard foods) at the same rate as they grow. However, if the hamster is not supplied with material on which it can gnaw, or if it is suffering from a hormone imbalance, its teeth may grow faster than they are worn down. In some cases, the teeth may grow so large that the hamster cannot eat, as the teeth block the mouth. Obviously, if medical attention is not forthcoming, the affected hamster will die a long, slow and painful death from starvation. For this reason, teeth must be checked regularly and, if they are too long, they need to be clipped.

When a hamster's teeth are misaligned, such as when the growing area in the gums is affected by injury or infection, one or more of the teeth may grow out of line, therefore not meeting the opposing teeth. This can cause overgrowth and, once one tooth is out of line, the other follows. As the teeth of all rodents grow at such a fast rate, regular (i.e. monthly) checks and clipping are needed, if this problem occurs.

This is a painless operation for the hamster *provided* that it is carried out by a person with sufficient knowledge and experience. Most vets will be pleased to demonstrate the action to serious fanciers, but do not attempt this operation until you have been shown the correct and safe way.

Salmonellosis

Salmonella infection may cause diarrhoea or simply a loss of weight and condition (with or without diarrhoea). Such infections are easily transmitted to other species *(including humans)*, and so extra care should be taken. Wash your hands thoroughly after handling infected hamsters and ensure that you do not cross-infect other hamsters by lack of basic hygiene.

Infected hamsters are best humanely destroyed, to avoid further infection in the hamstery. All cages of affected hamsters should be cleaned and washed using a strong disinfectant such as Jeyes Fluid. All bedding, shavings etc. from infected hamsters must be burned.

Shock

Clinical shock (or trauma) is an acute fall in blood pressure, and is often evident after the hamster has had a fall or a fight, or been injured in some accident. It will manifest itself with some or all of the following symptoms:

a) Cool skin and pale lips and gums (a result of poor circulation due to the drop in blood pressure),
b) Faint and rapid pulse,
c) Staring eyes.

The victim must be kept warm, and its blood pressure returned to normal as soon as possible. This may happen simply by placing the hamster in a warm, dark cage. It helps to massage it gently, to help the circulation, and to wrap it in a piece of towel to keep it warm. It must be kept warm and quiet, and medical advice sought as soon as possible. Medical treatment consists of subcutaneous or intraperitoneal injections of a warm electrolyte, such as Hartmann's solution; multi-vitamins and antibiotics may also be administered.

Skin diseases

Hamsters can suffer from three different types of skin complaint. Sometimes, the hamster (especially males) will show large patches of wet fur, or even baldness, on its hips. This is not usually a sign of illness or disease, merely the animal's hip spots showing.

Demodicosis

This disease involves one or two species of mite – *Demodex criceti* and *D. aurati*. In some hamsters, these ectoparasites can cause scaliness, papules and alopecia. The disease is more common in male hamsters than in females.

This condition requires veterinary treatment as soon as possible. Even after treatment, the condition can still recur. Improved hygiene and nutrition may prevent this condition.

Ringworm

This is a contagious skin disease caused by the growth of certain types of fungi on the skin of the hamster. It appears in the form of patches of dry, crusty skin. There are no hairs on these patches, which are scaly in appearance and usually circular. The ear pinnae are often affected.

Treatment consists of clipping, improved cage hygiene and the application of griseofulvin (administered by a veterinary surgeon).

Sarcoptic mange

Relatively rare, this is a highly contagious condition, caused by the mite *Sarcoptes scabei*. In human beings, this disease is known as scabies.

Hamsters can be treated, if medical care is sought at an early stage. Severely infected hamsters should be humanely destroyed. All cages must be thoroughly disinfected with an industrial strength disinfectant, and all bedding and shavings burned.

Some skin diseases are also caused by the harvest mite, present in hay supplied as bedding. Veterinary advice must be sought and all hay must be removed and burned. Even better, do not supply hay to your hamsters; use a top-quality paper-based bedding instead (but *not* newspaper).

Sleeper disease

Sometimes, when the ambient temperature gets too high and the hamster cannot cool itself, it may go into a state of immobility; this is known as 'sleeper disease' or heat stroke. The hamster will be stiff and apparently lifeless and, if handled, may tremble, moving its head from side to side. If returned to a cooler area, normal behaviour will be evident within 5–10 minutes.

Hamsters must never be left in areas such as window ledges, or in cars, in hot weather. Ensure that the hamstery has sufficient shade and ventilation in warm weather.

Stings

Insect stings and bites happen infrequently, and are usually due to flying insects finding their way into the hamstery, and thence into the hamster's cage.

Clip a little fur away from the area, so that you can actually see the problem. Wash the area with a saline solution or a mild antiseptic. If a sting is present, it should be carefully removed with tweezers, and then the area wiped with either cotton wool or a cotton bud dipped in alcohol (e.g. surgical spirit). Dry the area, and use an antihistamine spray or apply a wet compress to alleviate the irritation and swelling.

If the hamster has been bitten or stung in the throat or face area, it should be taken to a vet immediately, as reaction to such stings can cause the airways to become blocked, thus killing the hamster.

Tyzzer's disease

This is caused by a bacterium – *Bacillus piliformis* – carried by mice, and usually introduced to hamsters via infected food and/or bedding. It is highly contagious and the symptoms are lethargy, loss of appetite, diarrhoea and weight loss. This disease is acute, severe and usually fatal, especially in young stock and nursing mothers, and is exacerbated by stress.

Treatment is not usually successful, but consists of improving the animal's hygiene standards and the administration of oxytetracycline, along with fluid therapy.

Prevention consists of ensuring that no fouled bedding or food is purchased (one of the reasons for my recommending that hay is *not* used), and that all such items are stored in sealed, rodent-proof containers.

Wet tail

Wet tail (proliferative ileitis) is without doubt the most common serious disease in hamsters, responsible for the deaths of many hamsters each year. It manifests itself as a severe diarrhoea, with a moistening of the rear area of the hamster (hence 'wet tail'). The disease usually leads to the death of the hamster within 2–7 days.

This disease is a form of colibacillosis, and is triggered by stress. It is very common in young hamsters that have been bred in colonies. In advanced cases, it is very difficult (and often impossible) to treat, and so it is often best to have such animals humanely destroyed. Mild cases can sometimes be treated with neomycin, and the stress and dehydration which accompanies wet tail must also be treated. The latter is achieved by the use of subcutaneous injections of lactated Ringer's solution (a mixture of sodium, calcium and potassium chlorides) and multi-vitamin injections.

Note on antibiotics

In the U.K. and many other countries, antibiotics are only available from a veterinary surgeon, and they will only supply them when treating a sick hamster that requires such drugs. Hamsters cannot be given penicillin, streptomycin or D.D.T. and organophosphorous compounds, as they may prove fatal. Only sulphonamides, potentiated sulphonamides and chloramphenicol have been proven safe for use with hamsters.

HOSPITAL CAGE

Many injuries and diseases require the patient to be kept warmer than usual. There are several ways to achieve this. One is to place the cage in a warm area, perhaps under a thermostatically controlled heat lamp; another is to place the hamster and cage on a similarly controlled heat pad. Some breeders prefer to have a custom-built 'hospital cage'.

This consists of a cage, not necessarily of the same design as the standard keeping cages, into which is fastened a thermostat controlling the heater, surrounded by wire mesh to prevent the hamster from chewing the thermostat or wires. I use an aquarium, with three sides covered by hardboard. This covering serves several purposes: it helps insulate the cage from cold, heat, sound and light, and it also gives the hamster some privacy. The cage is topped with a well-fitting, ventilated lid, into which is fixed an infra-red heat bulb. The thermostat is set to 23–25°C (73–77°F), and the hamster is placed in this cage while it is undergoing treatment. Every serious hamster fancier should have at least one of these cages in his hamstery.

EUTHANASIA

There comes a time in a hamster's life where it would be cruel to allow it to continue to live. This may be when the animal is injured, sick, has a contagious or infectious disease, or the hamster may simply be so old that it has difficulty carrying out the day-to-day tasks of living. At such a time, it is necessary to destroy the hamster humanely. Euthanasia should not, however, be used as a method of disposing of unwanted or surplus stock. Carefully controlled breeding programmes should ensure that such a problem never arises.

Many breeders simply take their hamsters to the vet for an injection (an overdose of barbiturates). Some experienced breeders, however, prefer to do the job themselves. Obviously, it is not possible for the breeder to have access to injectable barbituates (and rightly so), and so he must use other methods. The prime concern here is to kill the hamster in a humane way, i.e. there should be no suffering or distress

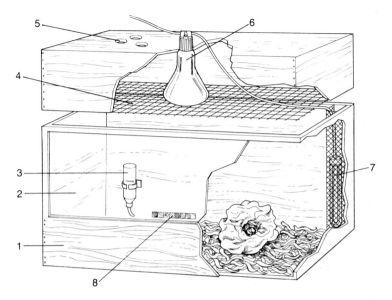

Fig. 22 Hospital cage: **1.** Wood cladding to give inmate privacy and insulate the cage from cold/heat and noise. **2.** Glass front. **3.** Water bottle. **4.** Wire-netting base to lid to prevent the hamster from climbing on heater. **5.** Ventilation holes. **6.** Ceramic heat bulb. This is better than a radiant heat bulb, as it will not disturb the sick hamster when the thermostat switches it on and off. **7.** Thermostat in wire cage (including electric cable) to prevent the hamster from gnawing on it. **8.** Thermometer.

for the animal (either physical or mental). The Universities Federation for Animal Welfare (U.F.A.W.) recommends chemical euthanasia using carbon dioxide. Again, it is unlikely that many breeders will have access to such material. Most breeders prefer to use dislocation of the neck. This can be achieved by a well-aimed blow to the base of the hamster's neck, but takes experience and courage to do correctly. Well before the need ever arises, you should seek advice from your own veterinary surgeon and, if you have any doubts at all about your ability to despatch a hamster without causing it undue suffering or stress, then you should not attempt to carry out the procedure yourself.

Euthanasia is to be used only to alleviate the animal's suffering, or to prevent the spread of disease to other animals.

As hamsters only live for 2–2½ years, if you can only prolong a life by a month, this is comparable to about 3 years in a human being, and so it is well worth seeking veterinary advice and treatment for all sick or injured hamsters. After all, they do give you so much pleasure that they are definitely worth the effort, aren't they?

CHAPTER 10

New Technology

Today, many items of new technology are available to the serious hamster fancier. These can, if used properly, make life much easier, alleviating the pressures of day-to-day maintenance, thereby giving the fancier more time to devote to his charges. I am well known as a gadget man, but I will only continue to use such items if they are really useful to me. The most valuable asset that anyone has is time; if, by using a 'gadget' I can save myself some time, I feel that I should do so. With all new equipment and procedures, however, one must remember that there is always a learning curve, and so it will take time and effort before one is fully conversant with the equipment or procedure; only when you are fully conversant with it will you begin to reap the benefits.

COMPUTERS

Many households now have a personal computer (P.C.), and this can easily be used to help run systems, store records and work out genetic problems. These computers may be in the form of desktop, laptop or even pocket computers (organizers). I find that an organizer, which can easily fit into a pocket, is extremely useful for recording details while one is actually in the hamstery. With suitable software, this information can be 'down-loaded' on to the P.C. back in the warmth of the home. Of course the P.C. itself is useless without the appropriate software and so the choice of this software must be given thought.

For record-keeping (stud, show results, financial aspects, etc.) some form of data base is needed. Some software, such as DBase 4, can be very complicated and give many more facilities than are necessary. The average hamster fancier may not have the time (or inclination) to learn all of the many features which this software offers. As it is also quite expensive (costing about the same as a large shed suitable for an entire hamstery), it is also doubtful that fanciers will be buying a copy solely for this purpose. However, if you are in business, or have bought the software for another purpose, then you will find it

Three methods of recording stud details: a notebook, a pocket computer ('organizer'), and a laptop computer.

extremely useful. By using its facility to enable you to write your own programs, you can tailor them exactly to your purposes.

First Choice is a package which includes a data base, word-processing and spead-sheet facilities. I particularly like this software for its 'form-making' abilities. It enables the operator to design his own blank standard form (e.g. pedigree, breeding record etc.). The computer then stores both the blank and completed forms, enabling the operator to refer to records already written up (changing or adding to them if necessary), as well as displaying a blank form for completion if the operator wishes. All records are automatically cross-referenced by the computer.

All records kept on computer have the advantage of being easily accessible provided that some thought is given to their format, the fields chosen and their storage. Even if your P.C. has a hard disk, it is still essential that you 'back up' your information (and software) after every use of the P.C. Ideally, you should have the original software, a copy loaded on to your hard disk and a back-up copy. Every item of information that you input to your P.C. should also be stored on hard disk, with two back-up copies, one of which is best stored in a separate building from the other. This is merely for insurance against fire or other such damage. There is also a risk that a hard disk will 'crash' and lose all of the information stored on it. While this is certainly not an everyday occurrence (thank goodness!), it does occasionally happen and, if you have not backed up your files, then you will be in a sorry state. Such a crash can cause you to lose all of the information that you have gathered over many years, and so backing up should be made into a habit and carried out after every time that you use your computer.

Remember also to keep all floppy disks away from sources of magnetism, since the information on them is stored by using magnetism, and external sources can corrupt the information, rendering it useless. Televisions, hi-fi speakers and video-recorders are just some of the everyday items that are also powerful sources of magnetism.

P.C.s are also suitable for operating security systems and switching lights and other such items. Again it is necessary for suitable software to be purchased. Consult your dealer for suitable packages. The problem with using a computer for this type of application, however, is that the computer needs to be switched on for the entire time that the systems are required, which is usually 24 hours every day. If there is a power failure, the computer will crash or at least go off-line, and so the systems will fail. To avoid this, you can purchase an uninterrupted power supply (U.P.S.), but this is very expensive and can only keep the computer running for a few hours at the most. It is extremely difficult to justify the time, effort and money that such a computerized system will cost, but the decision is yours.

AIR CONDITIONING

True air conditioning is beyond the scope of this book and is not necessary for the hamstery. However, a form of temperature control is well worth the effort and cost of installing in a hamstery. My own system consists of two thermostats, one set at the minimum temperature to which I want the inside of the hamstery to drop, the other at the maximum to which I wish the temperature to rise. The thermostat set at the minimum temperature is wired to operate a heater, switching it on when the temperature drops to a pre-determined level, and off again when it has risen above that level.

The thermostat set at the maximum temperature required is wired to operate an extractor fan. The idea is that, when the temperature rises (e.g. in hot weather), the extractor will prevent the temperature inside the hamstery from rising to a dangerous level. It is best to have a fan extracting hot air, rather than one pushing in outside air. The action of air being extracted will also bring in cooler air from the outside, while the opposite is not always so. Obviously, the margin

Three pieces of modern technology that will be useful in any hamstery *(from left)*: a time switch for controlling the light in the hamstery, giving long days and short nights; a combined automatic electronic air-freshener and fly-killer; and a thermostat to control an electric heater.

between the two has to be carefully set to prevent both systems operating at the same time, i.e. the heater warming the hamstery to such a degree that the extractor fan is switched on. This will merely result in huge electricity bills! In the winter, the extractor system can, if required, be isolated although, if the system has been correctly set up, this should not be necessary.

Unless you are fully conversant with electrical installation, do not attempt to install this system yourself. If the wiring is incorrectly installed there may be a risk of fire and consequent danger to life. All such work must be carried out by a qualified and experienced electrician.

FIRE PRECAUTIONS

Fire is a potential hazard in all homes and buildings. It therefore makes sense to try to reduce the risk of fire itself and also, to try to ensure that, if there is a fire, you can limit the damage done.

A smoke alarm will emit an audible warning in the event of a build-up of fumes, such as in a fire. This will alert you to the danger, enabling you to act to save the situation. You should also have at least one suitable fire extinguisher in the hamstery (of the correct type), and be conversant with the technique of using it. Do not wait until an emergency before you decide to read the instructions! A fire blanket may also prove useful.

Prevention of fires covers such items as a smoking ban in the hamstery itself, and all electrical installations being carried out in a safe manner, conforming to all safety standards. Care must also be taken to prevent any bedding or shavings being kicked out of cages and falling on heat sources such as a fan heater. Radiant heaters and those using naked flames must never be used in hamsteries.

SECURITY

As stated earlier, P.C.s can be programmed to operate security systems. However, I do not think that many fanciers will go to that length to secure their hamstery. A good burglar-alarm system can, nevertheless, be installed for quite a small outlay. I recommend such action as, quite apart from the monetary aspects of a break-in (items/ animals stolen, damaged or killed), the upheaval that this can cause can easily disrupt a breeding programme to the extent that the breeder will need to start over again – a daunting task, especially to someone who may have been developing a line over many years.

The alarm system itself does not have to be complicated. All that is required is a proximity switch on every door and window that opens, all linked to a very loud audible alarm – a siren is ideal. Fitting a flashing strobe light in the circuit and attaching it to the roof of the building in question will ensure that, if and when the alarm goes off, neighbours and police will be in no doubt as to where the problem lies.

If you use a self-contained 12V system, with a mains trickle charger to keep the lead-acid accumulator topped-up, you will still have an alarm during power cuts and when a potential burglar cuts the mains power to your hamstery. Use a key-operated switch and, most important of all, always remember to set the alarm *every time* that you leave the hamstery. Murphy's Law dictates that, on the one occasion when you fail to set the alarm, you will be visited by two-legged vermin!

Do not test the equipment without first informing neighbours (for obvious reasons) and, if the system should prove defective and cause false alarms, it should be serviced and repaired before it is used again. After a couple of false alarms, people will begin to ignore the alarm altogether and you will not be the most popular person in the area if you cause your neighbours to lose sleep. You should, therefore, inform neighbours if you have been having such a problem, apologizing for any inconvenience caused, and also inform them when you have had the problem cured, so that they will know that, the next time they hear the alarm, there really is a problem!

FOOD STORAGE

All food needs to be stored in cool, dry conditions. For many types of food, air-tight containers will suffice. These may be of the plastic variety sold for the purpose, or may be empty coffee tins and jars. Whichever you use, ensure that you label the container clearly with the contents; a 'use by' date is also useful, helping to reduce the risk of feeding stale and old foods to the hamsters.

Fruit and vegetables need better storage than this, and so a refrigerator is needed. While most breeders will be content to use the family 'fridge, many will not be happy at the prospect of storing mealworms and other such hamster food items alongside their own food. For this reason, I recommend that, if possible, you should have a refrigerator specifically for your animals' foods.

This need not be large or expensive, but should be big enough to take enough fresh food to last the hamsters for at least 7–10 days. It is also useful to store a container of water in this 'fridge, especially during hot weather. This cold water can then be used to top up the drinking water for the hamsters, thus helping them keep cool.

AUTOMATIC WATERING SYSTEMS

Many (probably most) hamster keepers use individual water bottles for their stock. This can, though, be very time-consuming in that each and every bottle has to be filled and refilled at regular intervals and all individually. Today, there are several systems which use just one header tank and tubes and valves to take water to every cage in the building.

These systems consist of lengths of rubber or plastic tubing which can be cut to suitable sizes and linked together using metal or plastic joints. These are usually in the shape of a T. Through the top of this T passes the main water supply, while the other opening has a short piece of tubing attached. At the end of this is a metal valve system, which is fixed into the hamster's cage and from which the hamster drinks. Every valve has its own removable filter and a further filter may be fixed at the beginning of the system. The header tank will need to be at least 50–100mm (2–4in) above the top of the highest tank to give it sufficient head to function correctly.

Qualities to look for in such systems include: black tubing, to limit the amount of light (and hence algae growth); stainless steel fittings; a valve that allows the animals to take the amount of water that it requires without any backflow (backflow can allow cross-infection of stock, i.e. germs from a diseased animals can find their way into the watering system and thence to other stock sharing that watering system).

Most require only a smallish header tank, which needs to be more than 40–50mm (1½–2in) above the actual valves. The valves use a mechanical lever, thus ensuring that they are kept closed when not being used by the animals.

IONIZERS AND ION PROBES

An ionizer emits a stream of negatively charged ions which help to 'freshen' the air, causing airborne particles to settle. As such, they reduce dust and airborne infection. These items cost very little to buy, and even less to run, and I recommend them to all keepers of small livestock.

There are two main types of ionizers – ones that come in neat boxes and are plugged into a standard three-pin power socket and those which simply plug into a wall or roof socket designed for light bulbs. Both operate in the same way and the choice is purely personal.

They have two main effects: the ions combine with airborne particles of dust, dirt and smoke, and they are then attracted to the nearest earthed surface by electrostatic action. This earthed surface may be a table, a ledge or a shelf. In this manner, all such particles are removed from the air of the hamstery. These airborne particles may also be bacteria and fungal spores, which can of course cause disease and illness in the hamsters.

Negative ions also seem to have an effect on the way that animals react, in that the animals seem to perk up almost visibly when an ionizer is switched on in their room. Scientists believe that negative ions reduce stress hormones and, as stress is probably the major contributory factor in the deaths of most captive animals, this is extremely beneficial to stock.

Three more items of 'high-tech' that will be useful in the modern hamstery *(from left)*: an ionizer; a smoke detector; and a controlled light.

INTERCOMS

Where the hamstery is situated a distance from your home, you may find it beneficial to install an intercom. There are several makes on the market today which are simply plugged into the electric sockets and, provided that both sockets are on the same system, no further wiring is required. Indispensable where you (like me!) tend to get carried away and stay in the hamstery for longer than you really ought to. With an intercom, you can be reminded that dinner is now cold!

Such intercoms are sold for monitoring babies, often being called 'baby alarms'. They are relatively cheap and a good investment.

FLY-KILLER AND AIR-FRESHENER

Most insecticides cannot be sprayed in the hamstery while it is occupied, as the danger of contamination of food and hamsters is too great. However, today's market has several devices which can automatically dispense insect-killing material and/or air-freshener which is perfectly safe (i.e. to food hygiene standards). These devices measure about 200mm × 100mm × 70mm (8in × 4in × 2¾in), and consist of an electrically operated fan and two containers – one for the air-freshener, the other for a specially formulated solid insect-killing strip. The device has three settings: off, on continuously and on intermittently. The latter is the setting which will be of most interest to hamster keepers. On this setting, the fan operates for about one minute in every ten.

The fly-killer should be positioned in the hamstery so that it does not blow straight at or on to the cages, as a safeguard. Place it high up and replace the insecticidal strip at intervals recommended by the manufacturer.

It is all too easy to spend vast amounts of money on 'gadgets' and great care and thought should be given before any such purchases are made. On the other hand, some of these items of new technology can save you time and make your life easier, providing that you are prepared to give time and effort to learn how to use the equipment to its full potential.

Keep an open mind and, if you feel that a certain piece of equipment would help you, buy it, learn how to use it properly, and make life easier for yourself!

CHAPTER 11

Wild Hamsters in the U.K.

The Syrian hamster has proven to be remarkably adaptable and there have been reports of wild or 'feral' colonies of these animals appearing in different parts of the world. In the U.S.A., the authorities were so worried that, until 10 February 1948, hamsters were forbidden entry into the U.S.A. at least for the general public or as pets (exceptions were made for laboratories and other such institutions). In 1948, Albert Marsh, the States' first hamster entrepreneur, persuaded the authorities to allow laboratory reared hamsters to be afforded the status of a 'normally domesticated animal'; hamsters could, therefore, be kept as pets by the general public.

The American authorities were acting to try to prevent the Syrian hamster from becoming a pest in their country, and who can blame them when one considers the way that non-indigenous animals like the rabbit were allowed into Australia. Today, the rabbit is classed as an agricultural pest in Australia and literally thousands are killed – shot, poisoned, gassed and snared – each year. This has not, however, prevented the rabbit population from reaching plague proportions. Australia has learned its lesson and, today, very few species of non-indigenous animals are allowed into that country. The Syrian hamster is still absolutely *persona non grata* in Australia!

There have been many instances (mostly not recorded in detail) of hamsters escaping into the wild and colonizing areas in many parts of the world, but there is no room in the scope of this book to cover them all in detail – even where such detail is available. However, the following examples of escapes in the U.K. will illustrate the potential problem. One should also bear in mind that, if hamsters can live wild in the far from hospitable climate found in the U.K. (when the animals originated from a desert area), then they are adaptable enough to live almost anywhere!

RECORDED ESCAPES

Bath, Somerset

In August 1958, rodent-control officers of the Bath Public Health Department were called to a pet shop, in an old part of the city, to investigate what was thought to be a rat infestation, which had been reported by the pet-shop owner and the owner of a greengrocery store on the opposite side of the street. Both shops had suffered from damage to food items in their stock, stored in the basements of the shops. On investigation, the council officers discovered several small holes between the bricks in the walls of the basements. A phosphorous poison and Warfarin (a blood anti-coagulant) were put down in the area, and this disappeared although no bodies were ever found.

On being questioned by the rodent-control officers, the pet-shop proprietor admitted that six Syrian hamsters had gnawed their way out of the wooden cage in which they were being kept about 12 months previously. Two days later, on 13 August 1958, council officials set 18 break-back traps in the basement of the pet shop, baited with cauliflower (one of the most frequently eaten vegetables from the greengrocery shop across the road). In the first week, 40 hamsters were caught in these traps! By the end of August, only a further four hamsters were caught, and none at all during the first eight days of September. Consequently, believing the infestation to be at an end, council workmen filled the entrances to the holes on 8 September, re-opening them on the night of 22 September, at which time the traps were again set. One hamster was caught on 26 September and another on 2 October, but no more were caught, and so the holes were sealed up again.

Six other hamsters were also caught – four by the owner of the greengrocery shop, one after it had fallen into an empty dustbin in a house near to the pet shop (this one was captured alive), and one which was trapped in a nearby butcher's shop. Of the 48 hamsters taken by rodent-control officers (the only ones to be sexed and recorded), 20 were males and 28 were females. It is assumed that the poison that had been set before the traps had simply been carried away by the hamsters in their pouches, and had never been eaten, since extensive searches failed to find any evidence of dead hamsters.

Finchley, Middlesex

In August 1960, four hamsters were reported as having escaped from their cage in a pet shop in Finchley. Two individuals were running in the shop about 6 months later and, on i obvious evidence of digging and burrowing was found bay windows of the shop. Large amounts of food, including sunflower seeds and grain, were also found in the area. Traps and poison was set and, over a 9-month period, more than 20 hamsters were captured or poisoned to death.

All of the entrances to the hamsters' burrows were blocked in mid-November 1961 but, in March 1962, a child found a feral hamster in the road by the pet shop. Traps and poisons were again set and a further two hamsters were caught, both inside the pet shop.

Barrow-in-Furness, Cumbria

A pet-shop owner in Barrow-in-Furness reported what he believed to be a rat burrow in the cellar of his shop. On investigation, rodent-control officers found two hamsters and, on questioning the pet-shop proprietor, they discovered that six hamsters had escaped from a cage in the pet shop a few weeks previously. The burrow was filled in and no other hamsters were found.

Bootle, Merseyside

In 1962, a florist in Bootle reported that large amounts of flowers in the shop had been damaged by rodents. Traps were set, and 17 hamsters were caught; it is thought that they had escaped from the pet shop adjacent to the florist's shop.

Manchester

In 1964, Manchester's Public Health Department investigated an infestation of rodents in a row of five terraced properties (one of them a pet shop) in the town centre. An unknown quantity of hamsters was found living in the buildings and all were destroyed. The obvious conclusion drawn by the Council's rodent-control officers was that the hamsters had escaped from the pet shop some time earlier in the year.

Bury St Edmunds, Suffolk

Early in 1964, a pet-shop owner in Bury St Edmunds noticed evidence of a rodent infestation and found tunnels under the cellars of the property. These tunnels were found to be extensive and three barrow-loads of earth and mortar were later taken away from the area. Traps and poisons were set and over 70 hamsters were caught. The colony had also spread to other rooms in the building, making their nests around electricity cables and light fittings.

Still more animals were caught later in the year; in all 230 feral hamsters were caught or killed in and around the pet shop.

Barnet, London

In the autumn of 1981, a large infestation of Syrian hamsters was found in council houses, garden allotments and tool sheds on a council housing estate at Hook Walk, Burnt Oak, Barnet, northwest London. Traps and poisons were set and some locals even hunted the hamsters, using air rifles to shoot them!

Even the extreme winter of 1981–82 did not keep the numbers of these feral hamsters under control, because they were seen in hordes throughout 1982. It is not known how many hamsters were killed by council rodent-control officers, nor is there any accurate record of the total number killed. Locals, however, claimed to have killed over 200 by their own efforts. If this is true, then it would suggest that the total feral population in the area may have been as high as 1000 or more! The media had a field day, and several national newspapers and television programmes featured the 'hamster invasion'. The backlash was that some hamster breeders were treated with distrust by members of the public for some time after the event.

The information in this chapter should convince you that the Syrian hamster really is hardy and quite capable of adapting to life under adverse conditions. It should also illustrate how easy it is for hamsters to escape and so you will appreciate how important it is to ensure that your hamsters are not allowed to escape or, if they do, that they are recaptured as soon as possible.

It is an offence in most countries (in the U.K. under Section 14 (1) of the Wildlife and Countryside Act (1981)) to release deliberately any non-indigenous species into the wild, or to allow such animals to escape due to negligence. You have been warned!

Hamster Facts and Figures

General information

Average lifespan   2-3 years
Average litter size   6 pups
Maximum litter size   20+
Average weight (adult female)   215g (7½oz)
Minimum breeding age (i.e. age at which mating is first possible)   28 days
Minimum recommended breeding age   4–6 months
Gestation period   15–17 days
Oestrus cycle   4 days
First indications of colour (goldens)   3–4 days
Ears begin to erect   3–4 days
*Ears begin to darken (goldens etc.)   7–8 days
Teats visible on females   7–8 days
Pups eat first solids   8–10 days
Eyelids visible   9–10 days
Eyes open   12–14 days
Pups first emerge from nest   13–15 days
Weaning age   28–32 days
Respiration rate   74 per minute
Pulse rate   450 per minute
Rectal temperature   36–38°C (96.8–100.4°F)
Chromosome number   44 (i.e. 22 pairs)

*Ears darken on dark-eared albinos at 42–50 days.

Average body weights

Males				Females		
Age (in days)	Weight (g)	(oz)		Age (in days)	Weight (g)	(oz)
1	3	⅛		1	3	⅛
21	40	1½		21	41	1½
42	85	3		42	93	3¼
84	105	3¾		84	115	4
108	141	5		108	160	5½

Hamster A–Z

Adler, Saul Commissioner of the expedition responsible for the capture of Syrian hamsters in 1930.

Aharoni, Israel The first Hebrew zoologist, and leader of the expedition which found Syrian hamsters on 12 April 1930.

Albino A white hamster with no pigmentation in its flesh or eyes. The eyes are opaque but, due to the fact that blood can be seen behind the eyes, they appear pink. There is no true (genetic) albino in hamsters. (*See also* Dark-eared albino.)

Aleppo The town in Syria around which live wild Syrian hamsters. The area that these wild hamsters occupy is very small, and they are not found anywhere else in that country.

Angora Long-haired.

Anopthalmic Without eyes, or only vestigal eyes.

Autosomes Chromosomes other than those which determine the sex of the progeny of a mating.

Bedding The material supplied to the hamster for its nest.

Benching The act of placing hamsters on the show bench, for the attention of the judge officiating at that show.

Ben-Menachen, Dr Hein First person to breed from the Syrian hamsters found in April 1930.

Cage The container in which hamsters are kept. This can be commercially manufactured, for pets or laboratory use, or home-made by breeders, using thick wood, plastic or metal.

Cannibalism The killing and eating of a hamster by another hamster.

Carbohydrates Food constituents which provide the body with energy.

Carrying box A container designed to hold several show pens, ideal for travelling or transporting the show pens to and from a vehicle. Sometimes called a travelling box.

Cheek pouches The pouches on the side of a hamster's head that it uses for carrying food, bedding etc. Females may also use these pouches for the transport of their pups. These cheek pouches are dry, unlike the cheeks of human beings.

Chromosomes Thread-like bodies, carried inside the nucleus of every cell, which bear the genes of the individual animal.

Class At a hamster show, entries are divided into classes, to facilitate judging. These classes are usually dictated by colour, variety or sex of the hamster concerned.

Coitus The physical act of mating.

Colony   Term used to describe the keeping of a group of hamsters together, usually for commercial breeding purposes, where one male is kept with several females. Hamsters kept in such conditions are invariably injured, sometimes fatally.

Crepuscular   The term used to describe an animal that is active around the hours of dusk and dawn.

Culling   The removal and killing of some pups in a litter which is thought to be too large for the mother to rear. This is totally unnecessary, as the female hamster will know her own limits, culling the litter as she sees fit, starting with the weakest members.

Dam   The mother of a litter.

Dark-eared albino   A white hamster with red eyes and grey, almost black, ears. This is not a true albino. (*See also* Albino.)

Deaton, Harry   One of the authors of the original *Hamster Handbook* (with T.W. 'Bob' Pond, 1956).

Dominant   A gene which will always show itself in the phenotype of a hamster, even if there is only one of these genes present. Such genes are denoted by the use of an upper case (capital) letter.

Ectoparasites   Parasites that live on the outside of an animal's body, e.g. fleas, lice and ticks.

Endoparasites   Parasites that live on the inside of an animal's body (e.g. in the intestines etc.), such as pinworms.

Exercise wheel   The wheel often supplied with cages for pet hamsters, into which the hamster will go and proceed to run round.

Fats   Constituents of food which provide the hamster's body with energy. A surplus of fats in a hamster's diet will cause it to become overweight, endangering its health.

Fibre   The indigestible material present in some foods which helps stimulate the action of the intestines. Used to be known as roughage.

Gene   A hereditary factor of inherited material. Genes are carried on the chromosome.

Genetics   The study of the ways in which certain characteristics are passed on from one generation to the next.

Genitals (Genitalia)   The external sex organs of a hamster.

Genotype   The genetic make-up of a hamster.

Genus   A group of animals containing species which are closely related to each other, e.g. the hamsters (*Cricetus*).

Germ cell   The egg of a female, and the sperm of the male hamster.

Gestation   Pregnancy. In hamsters, this is between 15 and 17 days, usually 16.

Golden   The original colour of the Syrian hamster. The colour is actually a golden brown, and *not* the colour of gold.

Golden hamster   Possibly a reference to the Syrian hamster, but more usually used to refer to any member of the species, i.e. *Mesocricetus auratus*.

Hamstery   The name given to the room or building in which hamsters are kept.

Heat   A term often used to describe oestrus. (*See also* Oestrus).

Heat stroke   *See* Sleeper disease.

Hibernation   The condition in which some animals pass the winter in a comatose state. Accurately speaking, the hamster does not hibernate.

Hip spots   The glands on the hips of all hamsters. More easily seen on the male, these glands are used to mark out its territory.

Hospital cage A special cage for sick or injured hamsters, fitted with a thermostatically controlled heater.

Hybrid A cross-bred hamster, i.e. heterozygous. The term is sometimes used to refer to the progeny of a mating of a closely bred animal and a completely unrelated one.

Hybrid vigour The increased vigour and resistance to disease often found in the offspring resulting from the mating of completely unrelated hamsters.

Inbreeding The practice of breeding very closely related hamsters together. (*See also* Line-breeding.)

Incinerator A device for burning rubbish in. Essential for the safe disposal of bedding and shavings etc. from the cages of infected and ill hamsters.

Incisors The front teeth of a hamster; these grow perpetually, maintaining their sharpness.

Inheritance The manner in which certain characteristics are passed from one generation to the next.

Intractibility Lack of tameness; impossible to handle without the risk of being bitten.

Judging board or frame The wire frame on which a judge places a hamster in order to study the hamster's appearance.

Kindle When a hamster is pregnant, she is said to be 'in kindle'; also the act of giving birth.

Life expectancy *See* Longevity.

Line A 'family' of hamsters, bred for several generations.

Line-breeding A moderate form of inbreeding.

Litter The young hamsters produced at one birth.

Locus (plural loci) Position on a chromosome occupied by a specific gene.

Longevity Length of life. In the hamster, this is about 2 to 3 years.

Marsh, Albert Founder of the Gulf Hamstery (U.S.A.), author of *The Hamster Manual*, and the person responsible for establishing the Syrian hamster as a pet in the U.S.A.

Mating *See* Coitus.

Mealworms The larval form of the meal beetle.

Mendel, Gregor The Austrian monk who first carried out and recorded experiments on the way in which certain characteristics are transmitted from one generation to the next.

Minerals Minute constituents of a hamster's diet, without which it will not have a balanced diet, with a consequent adverse effect on its health.

Mixed grain The term commonly used to describe a mixture of various seeds, grains, nuts and pulses often sold as hamster food. Accurately speaking, the term should only be used to describe a mixture of various grains.

Monohybrid inheritance The inheritance of a single characteristic.

Murphy, Michael First person known to have captured Syrian hamsters since 1930 (in May 1971).

Mutant or mutation The changed gene which results in a change in an animal; more accurately known as a mutant allele.

Nagging The hamster's action of continually gnawing on the bars of his cage.

Nocturnal The term used to describe an animal that is active by night, sleeping by day. (The hamster is more accurately described as crepuscular).

Nose rub A mark made on the hamster's nose, devoid of fur and caused by his nagging.

Oestrus The state in which a female hamster will accept a mating. (*See also* Heat.)

Oestrus cycle The sexual cycle of a female hamster (4 days).

Overshot A jaw in which the upper incisors overlap those on the bottom of the jaw.

Ovulation The release of eggs into the womb.

Parasites Animals which live on or in other animals (hosts) and are detrimental to the host, e.g. worms, fleas, mites, lice and ticks. (*See also* Ectoparasites; Endoparasites.)

Parlett, Bob and Jean The longest-serving members of the U.K. Hamster Fancy.

Parslow, Percy The man who founded the very first hamster farm, and became known as Mr Hamster.

Pen The old-fashioned term for a cage. Today, this term is usually used to indicate the standard show pen.

Phenotype The physical appearance of a hamster.

Photoperiodism The dependence on the daytime/night-time ratio of various biological functions, particularly the commencement of oestrus.

Pond, T.W. (Bob) Co-author of the original *Hamster Handbook* (with Harry Deaton, 1956).

Pregnancy *See* Gestation.

Proteins The basic constituents of all living things, and a constituent of a balanced diet essential for growth and tissue maintenance.

Pup A baby hamster.

Recessive A gene which is masked unless another identical gene is present in a hamster. Such genes are denoted by writing their code in lower case letters.

Records All of the information concerning your hamsters. These records must always be kept and, of course, kept accurately.

Reynolds, H.W. Author of first book on Syrian hamsters (*Golden Hamsters*, 1947).

Robinson, Roy The U.K.'s leading authority on the genetics of the Syrian hamster.

Rodent A mammal possessing two pairs of perpetually growing and self-sharpening teeth.

Roughage *See* Fibre.

Russell, Alexander and Patrick Authors of the book *The Natural History of Aleppo*, in which first mention of the Syrian hamster is to be found (2nd edition, 1797).

Scours Diarrhoea.

Season *See* Oestrus.

Sex chromosomes The chromosomes responsible for determining the sex of a hamster. Males have one X chromosome and one Y. Females have a pair of X chromosomes. All other chromosomes are known as autosomes.

Sex-linked inheritance The term used to describe a characteristic where the mutant allele is carried on the sex chromosome and is, therefore, governed by the sex of the individual, e.g. yellow (tortoiseshell).

Sexual dimorphism The differences exhibited between the sexes, e.g. the female hamster always has the capacity to grow larger than the male; the male long-haired hamster always has the capacity to have longer hair than the female etc.

Show pen The standard cage in which all hamsters must be placed when they are benched for exhibition.

Sibling Brother or sister; littermate.

Sire The father of a litter.

Skene, James Henry Believed to be the first person to have brought and kept a colony of Syrian hamsters in the U.K. (1880).

Sleeper disease The effect of too much heat on a hamster. If this condition is not treated, it can be fatal. Also called heat stroke.

Split The term used to describe a hamster whose parents were of different varieties/colours i.e. a heterozygote.

Sport The term used to indicate a hamster which is genetically different from the norm.

Stand A female on heat will 'stand' for the male, thus accepting his mating.

Stud An individual hamstery. Most clubs allow one to register a stud prefix (name) which is exclusive to the registrant. Often used to describe the male hamster used for breeding purposes.

Stud book The record (not necessarily a book) of all of the hamsters in a particular hamstery.

Travelling box *See* Carrying box.

Undershot A jaw in which the lower incisors overlap those on the top jaw.

Variety A specific colour and coat type of the hamster, e.g. a satin long-haired dark golden.

Vaccination An injection of a mild form of a specific pathogenic micro-organism, which causes the body to form antibodies, thus helping to prevent the treated animals from acquiring a full dose of the specific disease. Not applicable to hamsters (yet!).

Vitamin deficiency The lack of certain important vitamins; this term is usually used to indicate the result of such a deficiency, rather than the actual lack of the vitamin(s) in question.

Vitamins Organic compounds, essential to the health of a hamster. Usually reffered to by letters of the alphabet, e.g. A,B,C, etc.

Water bottle The bottle, equipped with a stainless steel spout, in which a hamster is supplied with water.

Waterhouse, George Robert Curator of the Zoological Society of London, who presented the first specimen of the Syrian hamster to that Society (9 April 1839).

Weaning The change from a liquid diet (mother's milk) to a solid diet.

Wet tail A form of chronic diarrhoea, usually fatal, and highly contagious.

Zoonosis Disease capable of being transmitted from one animal species to another, e.g. salmonellosis.

Zygote A fertilized egg.

APPENDIX 3

Useful Organizations and Addresses

It is an almost impossible task to produce a definitive listing of all organizations of interest to hamster keepers throughout the world. I have, therefore, had to make the decision merely to list representative bodies in some of the countries that I know this book is destined for. Readers who need more detailed information will be able to obtain this at their local library, zoological society or veterinary surgery.

When writing to any of the following, please enclose a self-addressed, stamped envelope, as all voluntary organizations depend upon income from membership subscriptions. Funds are, therefore, at a premium. Some of the following groups have no paid staff; please bear in mind that honorary officers will, from time to time, change.

UNITED KINGDOM

General Welfare

The Association of British Wild Animal Keepers (A.B.W.A.K.)
c/o Penscynor Wildlife Park,
Cilfrew,
Neath,
West Glamorgan.

This Association was founded in 1974 to 'further a common interest in wild animals', the emphasis being placed upon the husbandry of wild animals in captivity. As such, A.B.W.A.K. is not specifically interested in hamsters, but members of the Association possess a wealth of knowledge and information on many animals, including the *Cricetidae*. The Association's journal, *Ratel*, is a superb publication and contains many articles that will be of interest to owners/breeders of hamsters. *Ratel* is only available to members of A.B.W.A.K.

British Small Animal Veterinary Association (B.S.A.V.A.)
5, St George's Terrace,
Cheltenham,
Glos. GL50 3PT.

British Veterinary Association
7 Mansfield Street,
London W1M 0HT.

People's Dispensary for Sick Animals (P.D.S.A.)
Unit 6b,
Ketley Business Park,
Telford,
Shropshire TF1 4JD.

Royal College of Veterinary
Surgeons
32 Belgrave Square,
London SW1X 8QP.

Royal Society for the Prevention of
Cruelty to Animals (R.S.P.C.A.)
The Causeway,
Horsham,
Sussex RH12 1HG.

Hamster clubs

As the officers of hamster clubs are
liable to change from time to time, it
is impossible for me to give names
and addresses in this book. However,
any interested party may write to me
(via the publisher), and I will forward
the letters to the secretary of the
appropriate hamster club. Please
enclose a self-addressed stamped
envelope with all such enquiries. The
address to which your enquiries
should be sent is:

Hamster Clubs,
c/o Jimmy McKay,
Cassell plc,
Villiers House,
41/47 Strand,
London WC2N 5JE.

Institutes and societies

Institute of Animal Technology
5 South Parade,
Summertown,
Oxford OX2 7JL.

Institute of Biology
20 Queensberry Place,
London SW7 2DZ.

Joint Advisory Committee on Pets
in Society
Walter House,
418–422 The Strand,
London WC2R 0PL.

Society for Companion Animal
Studies (S.C.A.S.)
New Malden House,
1 Blagdon Road,
New Malden,
Surrey KT3 4TB.

The Universities Federation for
Animal Welfare (U.F.A.W.)
8 Hamilton Close,
South Mimms,
Potter's Bar,
Middlesex,
Tel. 0707 58202.

Magazines

Members of hamster clubs will
receive a copy of the monthly journal
of the Fancy. These journals are only
available to members of hamster
clubs.

Fur and Feather
This magazine regularly has articles
of interest to hamster owners. It is
available, on subscription only, from:
Winkley Publishing,
37–39 Fylde Road,
Preston PR1 2XQ.

Pet Keeper and Fancier
This is a monthly magazine that
regularly contains articles of interest
to hamster keepers, as well as more
general articles on pets. It is available
from your local pet shop, or in case
of difficulties, direct from the
publisher:
Sandcroft Publishing,
P.O. Box 42,
Oswestry,
Shropshire SY10 8ZZ.

Ratel
This, the journal of the Association
of British Wild Animal Keepers, is
published monthly, and is only available to members. Full membership

details may be obtained from Mrs Kate Partridge, 2a Northcote Road, Clifton, Bristol BS8 3HB.

Wild About Animals
A monthly magazine covering all areas of wild and captive animals, this occasionally has articles on hamsters. Available from your local newsagent or, in case of difficulties, direct from the publisher:
Gong Publishing Group Ltd,
4–8 Ludgate Circus,
London EC4.

UNITED STATES

Institutes and Societies

Animal Health Foundation
8338 Rosemead Boulevard,
Pico Rivera,
California 90660.

Animal Welfare Institute
PO Box 3650,
Washington, DC 20007.

Humane Society of the United States
2001 L St. NW,
Washington, DC 20057.

Scientists' Centre for Animal Welfare
PO Box 9581,
Washington, DC 20016.

United States Department of Agriculture
Washington, DC 20250.

Magazines

Animal Lovers
PO Box 918,
New Providence,
New Jersey 07974.

Avian/Exotic Practice
Veterinary Practice Publishing Company,
PO Box 4457,
Santa Barbara,
California 93103.

Pet Business
5728 Major Boulevard,
Suite 200,
Orlando,
Florida 32819.

Pet News
44 Court Street,
Brooklyn,
New York 11201.

Today's Animal Health
Animal Health Foundation,
8338 Rosemead Boulevard,
Pico Rivera,
California 90660.

APPENDIX 4

Cage and Equipment Suppliers

U.K. SUPPLIERS

Biotech Consultants
Brook Street,
Alva,
Clackmannanshire FK12 5JJ,
Scotland.

Manufacturers of animal cages and ancillary equipment.

North Kent Plastics (N.K.P.)
Home Gardens,
Dartford,
Kent DA1 1ER.

Manufacturers of top-quality small-animal cages and ancillary equipment, including racks, automatic watering systems, drinking bottles, stainless steel spouts, food scoops, label holders and cleaning equipment.

North West Plastics Ltd
Parr Bridge Works,
Mosley Common Road,
Worsley,
Manchester M28 4AJ.

Manufacturers of humane mouse-traps.

Reliable Thermostat Company Limited
96 Main Street,
Bramley,
Rotherham,
South Yorkshire.

Manufacturers of hospital cages and ancillary equipment.

Rolf C. Hagen (U.K.) Ltd
California Drive,
Whitwood Industrial Estate,
Castleford,
West Yorkshire WF10 5QH.

Manufacturers of small animal cages, exercise wheels and carrying cages.

Shaws Pet Products Ltd
Weston Road,
Aston Clinton,
Aylesbury,
Buckinghamshire HP22 5EH.

Manufacturers and distributors of cages and other such equipment for pet hamsters and other small mammals.

Steetley Minerals Ltd
Retford Road,
Worksop, Nottinghamshire S81 8AF.

Manufacturers of cat litter.

Vetbed (Animal Care) Ltd
Unit 10,
Ashley Industrial Estate,
Wakefield Road,
Ossett,
West Yorkshire WF5 9JD.

Manufacturers of bedding materials.

Bibliography

There are many books on the subject of hamsters, and specifically their care in captivity, and I have tried to list as many as I can. This list is not, however, exhaustive and the inclusion of a title is not meant to imply any form of endorsement.

In the early days of hamster keeping, some of the more enthusiastic and enterprising breeders printed their own booklets, notes and even books, often in the basement of their home! For this reason, it is impossible to give full details of all the books mentioned here. Many of these earlier books are now sadly out of print, although it may be possible to borrow copies from public and zoological libraries. This may well prove difficult but, if you are successful, I am sure that you will find the results of great interest.

I am a great believer in reading as much on any subject as I can find, thus obtaining different perspectives, picking up tips and new ideas, and generally broadening my knowledge of a particular subject. I have, therefore, included some books which may not at first seem particularly relevant, but all are, to my mind, worth reading to obtain a broader picture and deeper understanding of the Syrian hamster, and its place in the scheme of things.

Alderton, D. (1986) *Hamsters and Gerbils* Salamander, London and New York.

Allcock, J. (1983) *Small Pets of Your Own* Sheldon Press, London.

Barrie, A. (1987) *Step by Step Book About Hamsters* TFH Publications, Berkshire and New Jersey.

Birkett, C. (1979) *Heredity, Development and Evolution* Macmillan Education, Basingstoke.

Bruce, H.M. and Hindle, E. (1934) 'The Golden Hamster' in *Proceedings of the Zoological Society of London* vol. 1

Clutton-Brock, J. (1987) *A Natural History of Domesticated Mammals* Natural History Museum, London.

Cooper, J.E., Hutchinson, M.F., Jackson, O.F. & Maurice, R.J., eds. (1985) *Manual of Exotic Pets* British Small Animal Veterinary Association, Cheltenham.

Corbet, G.B. & Hill, J.E. (1980) *World List of Mammalian Species* Natural History Museum, London.

Daglish, B. (n.d.) *Pet Keeper's Manual* Dent, London.

Deaton, H. & Pond, T.W. (1962) *The Hamster Handbook* (paperback edition) Pond Press (private publication).

Folk, G.E. Jnr (1984) *Hamsters* TFH Publications, Berkshire and New Jersey.

Fritzsche, H. (1982) *Hamsters* Baron's, New York and London.

Grzimek, O.B., ed. (1973) *Grzimek's Animal Life Encyclopedia* Van Nostrand Reinhold, New York.

Harrison Matthews, L. (1971) *The Life of Mammals* Volumes 1 and 2. Weidenfeld & Nicholson, London.

Hearne, T. (n.d.) *Care for Your Hamster* Collins, London (With RSPCA).

Hearne, T. (n.d.) *New Observer's Book of Pets* Frederick Warne, Middlesex, UK (distributed in the US by Viking Penguin Inc, New York).

Henwood, C. (1985) *Love Your Hamster* Foulsham, London.

Hoffman, R.A., Robinson, P.A. & Magalhaes, H., eds. (1968) *The Golden Hamster* Iowa State University Press, Iowa.

Holmes, S. (1985) *Dictionary of Biological Terms* Longman, London.

Honacki, J.H. & Kinman, K.E. (1972) *Mammal Species of the World* Allen Press, London.

Jordan, W.J. (1986) *A–Z Guide to Pet Health* Constable, London.

Knibb, S.M. (1982) *Smaller Pets* Robert Hale, London.

Lawrence, J. (1986) *Hamsters* Hamlyn, London.

Lawrence, J. & K. (1987) *Hamsters* Hamlyn, London.

Leftwich, A.W. (1967) *Dictionary of Zoology* Constable, London and D. Van Nosband, Princeton, New Jersey.

Lever, C. (1977) *Naturalised Animals of the British Isles* Hutchinson, London.

MacDonald, D., ed. (1984) *Encyclopedia of Mammals* Volume 2. Allen & Unwin, London.

Marsh, A.F. (1948) *The Hamster Manual* (self publication).

Martin, R.M. (1984) *First Aid and Care of Wildlife* David & Charles, Newton Abbot.

Morris, D. (1965) *The Mammals* Hodder & Stoughton, Sevenoaks.

Ostrow, M. (1982) *Breeding Hamsters* TFH Publications, Berkshire and New Jersey.

Palmer, J. (1983) *Small Pets* Blandford Press, Dorset.

Pardiso, N. (1983) *Walker's Mammals of the World* John Hopkins University Press, Baltimore and London

Parslow, P. (1967) *The Basic Facts of Practical Hamster Breeding* (self publication).

Parslow, P. (1967) *Percy Parslow's Hamsters in Colour* (publisher unknown).

Parslow, P. (1969) *Hamsters* Cassell, London.

Parslow, P. (1979) *Hamsters* TFH Publications, Berkshire and New Jersey.

Pinniger, R.S., ed. (1966) *Jones' Animal Nursing* British Small Animal Veterinary Association, London and Pergamon Press, Oxford.

Pond, T.W. (1965) *Golden Hamster* Ditchfields British Books, Leyland, Lancs.

Ravensdale, T. (1969) *Animals in Home and School* John Gifford, London.

Reynolds, H.W. (1947) *Golden Hamsters* Zoological Society of London, London.

Roberts, M.F. (1973) *How to Raise and Train a Pet Hamster* TFH Publications, Berkshire and New Jersey.

Roberts, M.F. (1987) *Complete Guide to Hamsters* TFH Publications, Berkshire and New Jersey.

Roberts, M.F. (1974) *Teddy Bear Hamsters* TFH Publications, Berkshire and New Jersey.

Roberts, M.F. (1982) *Hamsters as Pets* TFH Publications, Berkshire and New Jersey.

Robinson, D. (1979) *Exhibition and Pet Hamsters and Gerbils* Spur Publications, Saiga Publishing, Surrey.

Robinson, R. (1978) *Colour inheritance in small livestock* Fur and Feather, Preston, Lancs.

Robinson, R. (1973) *Right Way to Keep Hamsters and Others Rodents* Paperfronts, Kingsford, Surrey.

Russell, A. (2nd ed. 1794) *The Natural History of Aleppo* printed for G.G. and J. Robinson, London.

Schneider, E., ed. (n.d.) *Enjoy Your Hamster* The Pet Library, London.

Shaw, M. and Fisher, J. (1939) *Animals as Friends, and How to Keep them* Dent, London.

Siegel, H.I., ed. (1985) *The Hamster – Reproduction and Behaviour* Plenum Press, New York.

Smith K.W. (1976) *Hamsters and Gerbils* Bartholomew, Edinburgh.

Snow, C.F. (1972) *Hamsters* Foyles, London.

Spaulding, C.E. & Spaulding, J. (1979) *Complete Care of Orphaned or Abandoned Baby Animals* Rodale Press, Emmans, Pennsylvania.

Stonefield, M. (1981) *Hamsters, Gerbils, Rabbits, Mice and Guinea Pigs* Macdonald, London.

Universities Federation for Animal Welfare, ed. (1976) *U.F.A.W. Handbook on the Care and Management of Laboratory Animals* 5th edition. Churchill Livingstone, Edinburgh.

Watmough, W. (1978) *Practical Inbreeding* Watmoughs, Bradford.

West, G., ed. (1988) *Black's Veterinary Dictionary* 16th edition. A. & C. Black, London.

Young, J.Z. (1978) *The Life of Vertebrates* 2nd edition. Oxford University Press, Oxford.

Zoological Society of London (1964) *Longacre Book of Pets* Odhams Books, London.

Index